French is Fun at Key Stage 1

Activities, Games and Resources to Make Learning Fun

Florentina Popescu

We hope you enjoy using this book. If you would like further information on other books or resources published by Brilliant Publications, please write to the address given below or look on our website: www.brilliantpublications.co.uk.

Other books published by Brilliant Publications for teaching French:

Bonne Idée
Brilliant French Information Books
Brilliant Songs to Teach French Grammar
C'est Français
Chantez Plus Fort
French Festivals and Traditions
French Pen Pals Made Easy
French Speaking Activities
Fun French Fairy Tale Plays
Getting to Grips with French Grammar at KS2
Hexagonie – Part 1 and 2
J'aime Chanter
J'aime Parler

J'aime Beaucoup Chanter en Français
Jouons Tous Ensemble
Learn French with Luc et Sophie
Learn French Through Raps
Loto Français
Petites Étoiles
Physical French Phonics
Unforgettable French
100+ Fun Ideas for Teaching French across the Curriculum
12 Petites Pièces à Jouer
21 Fun Songs to Teach French Phonics

Published by Brilliant Publications Limited
Unit 10
Sparrow Hall Farm
Edlesborough
Dunstable
Bedfordshire
LU6 2ES, UK

E-mail: info@brilliantpublications.co.uk
Website: www.brilliantpublications.co.uk
Tel: 01525 222292

The name Brilliant Publications and the logo are registered trademarks.

Written by Florentina Popescu

© Text Florentina Popescu 2020
© Design Brilliant Publications Limited 2020

ISBN: 978-0-85747-830-6

The book and USB-card cannot be sold separately.

First printed in the UK in 2021

The right of Florentina Popescu to be identified as the author of this work has been asserted by herself in accordance with the Copyright, Designs and Patents Act 1988.

All rights reserved. Apart from any use permitted under UK copyright law, no part of this publication other than flashcards (pages 53–108) may be reproduced or transmitted in any form or by any means, electronic or mechanical, including photocopying and recording, or held within any information storage and retrieval system, without permission in writing from the publishers or under licence from the Copyright Licensing Agency Limited. Further details of such licenses (for reprographic reproduction) may be obtained from the Copyright Licensing Agency Limited, 5th Floor, Shackleton House, 4 Battle Bridge Lane, London SE1 2HX (https://cla.co.uk)

Credits

Rose and Pointé illustrations: Gaynor Barrs
0,1,2,3,4,5,6,7,8,9; Open Clipart Vectors: Pixabay
happy-birthday; DebiBrady: Pixabay
cake-5 candles; clker-free-vector-images: Pixabay
birthday; SandraSchön: Pixabay
Moon; GanapathyKumar: StockSnap
Mars, red planet;Wikilmages: Pixabay
Jupiter; Hphotostudio: Pixabay

Venus; Bruno Albino: Pixabay
Mercury; Bruno Albino: Pixabay
Saturn; Reimund Bertrams: Pixabay
Sun; Wikilmages: Pixabay
girl/dog; ClickerFreeArt: Pixabay
Fruit; Gred Altmann: Pixabay
Banana, Apple, Orange, Pineapple, Pear, Cherry; clker-free-vector-images: Pixabay
Various illustrations: Brilliant Publications

Contents

Introduction 4–5

Lesson Plans
1. Greetings 6–8
2. Introducing yourself 9–11
3. Numbers 0 to 10 12–14
4. How old are you? 15–16
5. Numbers 11 to 20 17–19
6. Colours 20–23
7. Days of the week 24–26
8. Animals and pets 27–29
9. Fruit 30–33
10. Months of the year 34–37
11. Parts of the body 38–40
12. Family members 41–44
13. Vegetables 45–48
14. Classroom instructions 49–51
15. Au revoir 52–53

Flashcards
Greetings 54–63
Introducing yourself 64
Numbers 0 to 10 65–70
How old are you? 71–74
Numbers 11 to 20 75–78
Colours 79–85
Days of the week 86–87
Animals and pets 88–93
Fruit 94–97
Months of the year 98
Body parts 99–100
Family members 101–103
Vegetables 104–105
Classroom instructions 106–107

© Brilliant Publications Limited   **French is Fun at Key Stage 1**

Introduction

Recent studies show that there is a 'critical age' when people can learn a language, whether native or foreign, with fluency and accuracy. The studies also show that a child is able to reproduce a variety of sounds, including foreign ones, starting at the age of 10–12 months. (*A First Language: the early stages*, Roger Brown, Harvard University Press, 2013). The younger the children are when starting to learn a language, the better they can reproduce the sounds – they pick up native accents effortlessly and with great accuracy.

French is Fun at Key Stage 1 enables you to teach French to young pupils in a way that will capitalise on their ability to pick up languages. The lessons contain a variety of games, music, pictures and actions, allowing pupils to be exposed to the French vocabulary again and again while having fun playing in the new language.

From experience, I have found that the best French lessons for Key Stage 1 (KS1) children:

- **Are active and varied**
Young children don't like to stay in one place for long. Each lesson should contain a variety of activities lasting no longer than 10 minutes each, with lots of opportunities for movement – whether it is moving from their table places to the carpet, wiggling their fingers or standing up and sitting down. Capitalise on pupils' spontaneity and lack of inhibition.

- **Are multi-sensory**
Present the French vocabulary in a variety of ways. Use the PPTs, flashcards and props to introduce the vocabulary so that children have a visual image to connect to the word. Where possible, teach actions to do with the vocabulary. You can involve children in coming up with actions for the new words. Clap the syllables as you say the words; this will help children to break longer words down and listen to the sounds. Repetition of vocabulary is essential for language learning. Make it into a game by using different voices (singing, chanting, speaking in a loud, soft, squeaky, spooky voice, etc).

- **Use props**
In addition to using flashcards, I have a supply of props that I use regularly:
    - Soft ball – ask children to pass a ball around the class, each saying a word when it is their turn
    - Small toys: animals, vegetables, fruit
    - Small bags – children love to pull something out of a bag; it adds to the excitement!
    - Puppets – use puppets to model French conversations. The puppets can speak with each other, with you and with the pupils.

- **Are fun!**
Pupils will love learning a foreign language through the use of games. Don't be afraid to play with the children and take them on an exciting adventure.

What is in French is Fun at Key Stage 1?

- **Lesson plans**

Each lesson comes already planned, offering a variety of choices for the specialist or non-specialist teacher. The order in which you teach the lessons, the steps you follow and the length of the lesson can be adjusted to suit your school and the needs and the abilities of the class.

There is enough material in *French is Fun at Key Stage 1* for all of KS1. As the number of lessons in the week and the length of the lessons varies from school to school, we have left it up to you, the teacher, to decide how long you spend on each topic. The lesson plans can be stretched over any number of sessions. In my experience children will have their favourite games and ask for these to be repeated.

With younger children you might wish to introduce just 4-5 words at a time and focus on learning vocabulary orally rather than presenting them with the written words, to avoid confusion as the children get to grips with English phonics. However, in my experience, children easily accept the fact that French phonics are different to English and presenting the written French words helps them to remember the vocabulary.

- **PowerPoint (PPT) presentations**

The PPTs provide audio and visual support for each lesson, with integrated audio files modelling the language. The vocabulary is presented both with images only and with words and images to give you flexibility.

Signing and singing are proved methods of learning language in an active and engaging way. Songs currently available on YouTube are signposted in the Extensions to each lesson.

- **Flashcards**

Many of the games use small flashcards and these are included at the back of this book. The flashcards can also be printed out in colour from the PDF of the book included on the USB drive.

Big flashcards are also helpful. The slides on the PPTs, both with pictures only and words and pictures, can be printed out, laminated and used to engage the pupils even more and to allow the teacher to practise the words with the class or group in a variety of ways.

In conclusion, *French is Fun at Key Stage 1* will benefit any teacher or school which would like to introduce a foreign language in their curriculum. The games and teaching suggestions can even be adapted to teach any language.

Enjoy learning and have fun. The secret is to let the child inside you take part in the lesson!

© Brilliant Publications Limited

French is Fun at Key Stage 1

1. Greetings

Introduction

Talk to the class about what you are going to teach today.

If this is their first lesson in French, ask them if they know any French words or anything about France. Give them some facts about France (showing them pictures). From my experience, the pupils love to be given information about the Eiffel Tower, croissants and famous French cheeses.

Explain that people who speak French do not just live in France, but also live in other countries around the globe, for example, Canada, Madagascar, Cameroon, etc.

Explain that today they will be learning to greet each other in French. Let the class know that by the end of this lesson you hope they can all answer the question *Comment ça va ?* (How are you?) in French.

Learning objective

To say simple greetings in French.

Vocabulary

Bonjour	Hello
Salut	Hi
Comment ça va ?	How are you?
Ça va bien	Good/I am good (well)
Ça va très bien	Very well/I am very well
Comme ci, comme ça	I am okay
Ça va mal	I am not good
Ça va très mal	I am not good at all
Désolé(e)	Sorry to hear this
Au revoir	Good bye

On the USB Drive

PPT presentation includes:
- actions with pictures only (slides 3–11)
- actions with words and spelling (slides 12–20)

Additional resources needed

Flashcards from PPT (slides 3–11)
Small flashcards with pictures only (pages 54–58)*
Small flashcards with pictures and words (pages 59–63)*
Small bag
Soft ball
Puppets

*Note: There are two versions of each small flashcard to enable pupils to ceate a conversation between Rose and Pointé.

Activity

1. Use the actions on the PPT presentation to introduce the vocabulary:

Bonjour / Salut	Waving	Hello / Hi
Comment ça va ?	Arms raised with palms splayed and shoulders hunched	How are you?
Ça va bien	Thumb up	I am good
Ça va très bien	Both thumbs up	I am very good

Comment ça va ?

French is Fun at Key Stage 1

© Brilliant Publications Limited

Comme ci, comme ça	Wobble hand from side to side	OK / I am OK
Ça va mal	Thumbs down*	I am not good
Ça va très mal	Looking ill, tongue out, thumbs down	I am not good at all
Désolé(e)	Sad face	Sorry to hear this
Au revoir	Waving	Goodbye

Ça va bien.

* Note: As Rose has multiple hands, the illustrator has chosen to use just one set for both *Ça va bien* and *Ça va mal*.

2. Make the pupils aware of the nasal pronunciation of *bien* and *comment*. A trick I use (that the children love), is to ask them to hold their nose when saying *bien* or *comment*. Then I ask them to try making the same nasal sounds, but without holding their noses.

Comme ci, comme ça.

3. Hold up the flashcards with pictures only or use the PPT slides, so you can practise saying the words on the vocabulary list a few times before showing the French spelling to the class.

4. Show the flashcards with words and pictures or the PPT slides. Explain to the class about the silent 't' in *salut/comment*. Explain that the final letter in most French words is silent. Show the 'ç' and explain that the little 'comma' is called a *cédille*. It is a sign which tells you that you have to pronounce the 'c' as a 's' (that's why is called *cédille*).

Ça va mal.

5. Put the children in groups of 4–5. Print out a set of flashcards with pictures only (one set per group). Call out a new word/ question/ answer and ask the pupils to hold up the card with the correct picture. After a few minutes of practice, choose a leader in each group (this should be a more able child) to call out the words, while the rest of the pupils show their cards.

6. Ask the children to help you to put the cards in a small bag. When they come to you to put the card in the bag, ask them *Qu'est-ce que c'est ?* (What is it?) Help the ones who struggle to remember.

Désolé !

7. Ask the class to sit in a circle on the carpet. Give them each a random card from your bag. Ask the pupils to look at their card and try to remember what their picture represents. Show the big flashcards with spelling again and ask the pupils only to watch and listen. Go around and collect the cards. They have to say what is on their card before putting it in your bag.

8. Give the class 5 or 10 seconds to return to their carpet spaces. (I prefer to count down in French right from my first lesson, but I explain beforehand that they will hear French numbers. Show the numbers on your fingers, so the pupils can see how many seconds are left.) Act out some conversations between the two puppets using the vocabulary, in front of the class. Ask them to listen carefully and to tell you at the

Ça va très mal.

© Brilliant Publications Limited

French is Fun at Key Stage 1

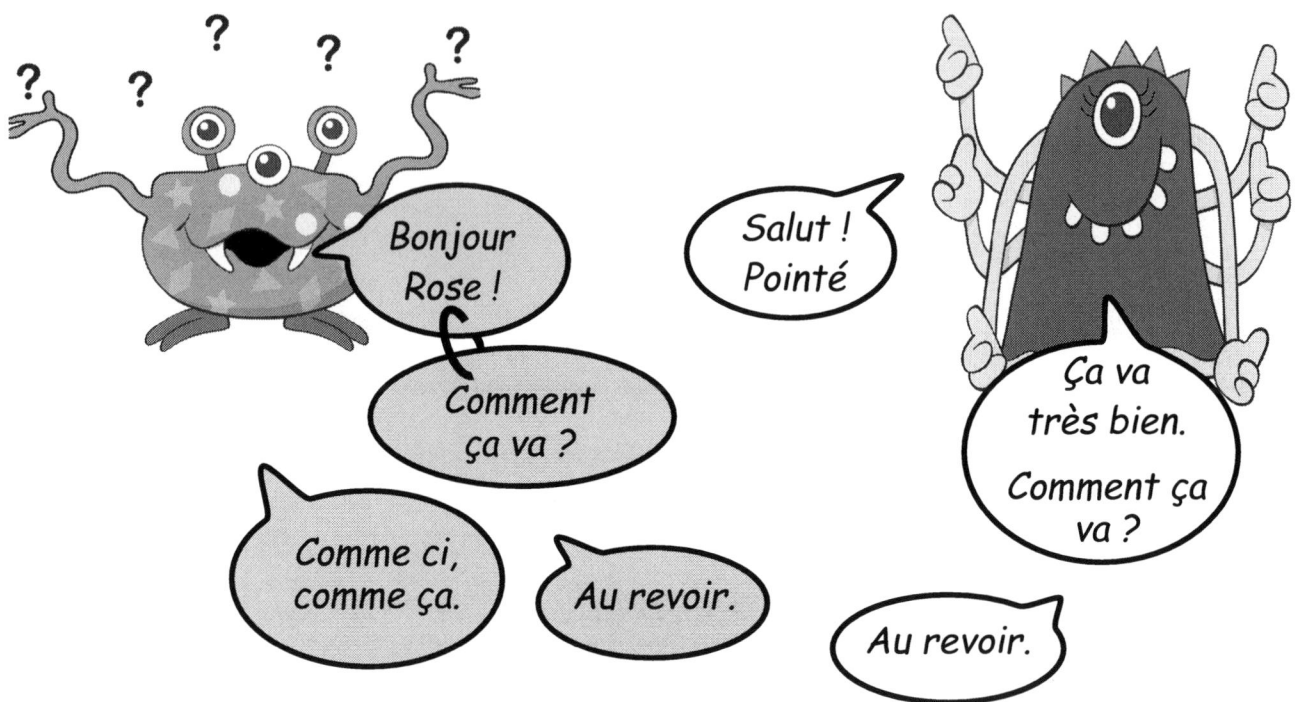

end of each conversation how your puppets are doing. I know from experience that the children absolutely love talking puppets.

9. Ask the pupils to sit in a circle and give them a soft ball. At the beginning, just ask them to pass the ball around, greeting each other with *Bonjour* or *Salut*. When they finish, choose a more confident pupil to ask the question *Comment ça va ?* and pass the ball to the next child, who should answer. Then he/she should pass the ball to the next child, asking the same question, etc.

10. Send the children to sit at their tables. Give out the little picture cards displaying the different answers to the question *Comment ça va ?* Ask three or four more able pupils to come to the front of the class. Give each of them a card with the question *Comment ça va ?* When you say 'Start', these pupils must go around each table and ask the question on their card. After each child has replied, they must collect the cards. The child with most cards gets a reward.

11. Play 'Magic chair' (I use the teacher's chair). The pupils must choose one of the answers to the question *Comment ça va ?* and keep it secret. Invite one child to come and sit on the 'magic chair'. The rest of the class then guess what he/she has chosen.

Ça va très bien.

Au revoir !

Extensions

Ask the class to watch and listen to the song *Bonjour, bonjour*, by Alain le Lait. Click on the link in the PPT (slide 21) https://www.youtube.com/watch?v=atNkI6QFZ50. Explain what the song says. Then practise the song with the class, asking them to stand up, dance and join in with actions. For now, practise only the target vocabulary: *bonjour, merci, comment ça va, très bien*.

French is Fun at Key Stage 1 © Brilliant Publications Limited

2. Introducing yourself

Introduction

Talk to the class about what they will be learning today and let them know that by the end of the lesson, you expect them to be able to ask and answer the question:
Comment t'appelles-tu ? (What is your name?)
Je m'appelle ... (My name is ...)

Learning objective
To ask someone their name and to answer in French.

Vocabulary

Comment t'appelles-tu ?	What's your name?
Je m'appelle ...	My name is ...
Enchanté(e)	Nice to meet you
Et toi ?	What about you?/ And you?
Monsieur	Mr
Madame	Mrs
Mademoiselle	Miss

On the USB Drive
PPT presentation includes:
- actions with words only (slides 3–7)
- actions with words and pictures (slides 8–12)

Additional resources needed
Flashcards from PPT (slides 3–7)
Small flashcards (page 64)
Soft ball
Puppets

For extension activity:
Print out some flashcards with famous characters for Extension C.

Activities

1. Start the lesson with a conversation, using your talking puppets to revise the previous French lesson, **Greetings**. Using funny voices, go around the class and choose some more confident children to talk to one of your French puppets, answering the question *Bonjour, comment ça va ?* Alternatively, replay the song they listened to in the previous lesson and ask them to join in, with actions and dancing.

   I always start my lesson by asking the class *Bonjour, comment ça va ?* followed by *Ça va bien ?/ Ça va mal ?/ Comme ci, comme ça ?* etc, using the appropriate hand signals for each one. The pupils will do the appropiate hand signal to show me how they feel, as I go through the list.

   They love it when I respond *désolée*, that's why most of them will be *ça va très mal !* at the beginning of the lesson – despite the big smiles on their faces.

Comment t'appelles-tu ?

© Brilliant Publications Limited

French is Fun at Key Stage 1

2. Sit the children in small groups on the carpet (4–5 pupils per group) and give them 5 minutes to practise the question *Comment ça va ?*, with all the possible answers. Choose a more able child in each group to ask his/her peers this question. Walk around making the pupils aware that you will be only listening when they practise, and you will be supporting the groups if they need you. If you have a TA, ask him/her to do the same. Walking and listening will give you a great opportunity to assess how well your pupils have learned the vocabulary.

3. Introduce the new vocabulary in this lesson using the PPT (slides 3–7) provided and talk to the class about the two aliens: Pointé and Rose.

4. Practise the question *Comment t'appelles-tu ?*. Remind the class about the nasal pronunciation of *comment* and about the silent 't' at the end. As this is a long question, practise first one word at a time: *comment... t'appelles... tu*. Then *comment t'appelles... tu*. After doing this a few times, try practising the whole question.

    You can clap your hands and ask the children to respond by clapping back and repeating *Co- mment- t'a- ppelles-tu ?* As this is a difficult question to remember, find different ways to practise it: clapping hands, funny voices etc.

5. Once the pupils are quite confident asking the target question, introduce *Je m'appelle ...* . Inform the children that their name stays the same as in English; they don't have to worry about their 'French name'. Make this clear straight after introducing '*Je m'appelle*', otherwise, they will be more interested in how to say their French names, rather than just answering the question *Comment t'appelles-tu ?* It is also very difficult to explain, at such an early age, that some names have a French equivalent and some don't (that could bring sadness or even some tears and you don't want this to happen).

6. Ask the children to make a circle around the carpet. Give one child a soft ball to be passed around the circle from one to another. As each child passes the ball, they should ask *Comment t'appelles-tu ?* The recipient child answers the question and then passes the ball to the next child asking the same question. Go round until everybody has asked and answered the question.

7. Divide the class in two. Ask the pupils to stand in two parallel lines, facing each other. Choose one line to start the game. The first child in this line should ask their opposite *Comment t'appelles-tu ?* That child should then reply *Je m'appelle ...* . The question is then asked by each child in the first line to their opposite until the end of the line is reached. Then swap over, so the other line of children asks the question.

8. Ask the class to listen to the song *Bonjour, salut, comment t'appelles-tu ?* which you can access by clicking on the link in the PPT (slide 13): (https://www.youtube.com/watch?v=PDiftkmK1-o) Get them to guess what *monsieur, madame, mademoiselle* mean. Explain the meanings and practise a couple of times with the class. I play a simple game

French is Fun at Key Stage 1

© Brilliant Publications Limited

with them and they love it. We practise by pointing at a boy and saying 'monsieur', at a girl, saying 'mademoiselle' and at the teacher/adult (if this is a lady, of course), saying *madame*. Then I call out one of the three new words and they must point at the right person.

Extension A

Ask the class to practise the new song by joining in only with:

Bonjour, salut, comment t'appelles-tu and *Je m'appelle*. Once the pupils are more confident, you can ask them to also join in with:

Bonjour monsieur, bonjour madame, bonjour mademoiselle.

Click on the link in the PPT (slide 13): https://www.youtube.com/watch?v=PDiftkmK1-o

Extension B

Using your talking puppets, practise a conversation in front of the class, as an example for the pupils:

Bonjour !	Salut !
Comment t'appelles-tu ?	Je m'appelle Pointé. Et toi ?
Je m'appelle Rose. Enchantée !	Enchanté !
Comment ça va ?	Comme ci, comme ça. Et toi ?
Ca va très bien, merci.	
Au revoir.	Au revoir !

Extension C

Print out some big cards with famous characters (Peter Rabbit, Cinderella, Winnie the Witch, etc). Ask the characters on your card *Comment t'appelles-tu ?* and answer with *Je m'appelle …* (+ the name of the character on the card). Put the small flashcards with famous characters in a bag, ask the pupils to sit in a circle and pull one card out of the bag. Go around to collect the cards. Ask each pupil *Comment t'appelles-tu ?* They have to answer with *Je m'appelle …* (+ the name of the character on the card).

This activity has never failed in my lesson and it is always great fun.

© Brilliant Publications Limited

French is Fun at Key Stage 1

3. Numbers 0 to 10

Introduction

Talk to the class about what you are going to teach today: numbers. Aren't they just great? Numbers help you to count your pencils, to measure how tall you are, to use the right quantities when making cakes, to count down, to play hopscotch or to help you count the money you have received from the Tooth Fairy. We are surrounded by numbers!

Learning objective
To learn the numbers 0 to 10 in French.

Vocabulary

zéro	=	0	six	=	6
un	=	1	sept	=	7
deux	=	2	huit	=	8
trois	=	3	neuf	=	9
quatre	=	4	dix	=	10
cinq	=	5			

On the USB Drive
PPT presentation includes:
- numbers without words (slides 3–13)
- numbers with words (slides 14–24)

Additional resources needed
Flashcards from the PPT (slides 3–24)
Small flashcards with pictures only (pages 65–67)
Small flashcards with words only (pages 68–70)
Numbers (plastic, magnetic or wooden)
Soft ball
Small bag

Activities

1. Ask the children to count for you in English, from 0 to 10. Play around with English numbers – maybe counting together in twos/ threes, or counting backwards from 10 to 0 etc.

2. After having first practised counting in English with the class, introduce the numbers in French. Then use funny voices and clapping hands to make different rhythms: *un* – clap once; *un, deux* – clap twice; *un, deux, trois* – clap x3, etc, *quatre … cinq … six* – clap x6. Always use visual support like cards, PPT slides, etc. Practise plenty of times with each number, in different ways. Show the numbers on the PPT (slides 3–13) then show the spellings (slides 14–24). It may be helpful to print out both versions of the PPT slides to make two sets of large cards, one with spellings and one without.

3. Choose a number. Show how many using your fingers, call it out and ask the class to repeat it, while copying your actions and your pronunciation.

4. Ask the class to stand up and follow you, marching around the classroom and calling out numbers. It's a fun way of moving and

zéro

un

deux

French is Fun at Key Stage 1

© Brilliant Publications Limited

learning at the same time, and the pupils love this. Of course, you have to think beforehand about the size and shape of the classroom, then decide if there is enough space to do this or if you would like to skip this step.

5. Put plastic (or magnetic/wooden) numbers in a bag and ask the children to take a number. Ask the children to organise themselves in numerical order and sit down individually in a circle. As each child sits, they must call out in French the number they are holding in their hands.

6. While the children are still seated and have their plastic numbers, ask them to hold up their number when they hear it being called out. Sing 10 Green Bottles but substitute the English numbers with their French counterpart. Encourage the children to join in.

7. Ask the children to sit in small groups on the carpet (4–5 per group) and give them the small cards with the numbers and the cards with the spelling. Give the groups 5 minutes to match the number with the numbers written out. (If you teach this lesson in Reception, use only number cards as pupils are too young to learn the spellings). Give one card to each child and ask them to remember what number is on their card. Call out the French numbers a few times. Ask the pupils to hold up the card when they hear their number.

8. Play a guessing game. Ask the children to choose one number from 1 to 10 and keep it secret in their head. Invite one more confident child to the front of the class and ask the rest of the group to guess the number he/she has chosen. The child who guesses the number comes to the front of the class and chooses another number.

9. Another game with huge success amongst my students is 'Class versus teacher'. It is a great game which goes well with any topic. Freeze the IWB on the slide with the numbers from 0 to 10 (slide 25). Count with the class first, pointing at each number. The class is now a team and they play against you. To keep score write on the board C (for class) and T (for teacher) and draw a short line down the middle. We usually play this game 3 times. The teacher chooses one number, which is 'the magic number' and lets the class know which number this is (make sure you repeat this number a couple of times before starting the game). The pupils have to stand up and repeat any numbers they hear you say, but if they hear 'the magic number', they have to be quiet and quickly sit down. As they are a team, they have to be well coordinated. If one single child calls out 'the magic number', then the class will lose the point. I try to make sure the class wins most times. Just occasionally do I score 1 point, just to 'save' my teacher pride. Once you have played this game and you know the rules, you can play this after teaching any other topic – the children will probably ask you to play this every single lesson.

10. The *Combien ?* slides on the PPT (slides 26–28) can be used as a mini-assessment.

trois

quatre

cinq

six

sept

huit

neuf

dix

Extension A

Talk to the class about the song they will be listening to. Explain that the song has only numbers up to 5, but it is a funny song about some elephants. Play the song once and ask the pupils to only watch and listen. Tell the class now that they will be listening to the song one more time, but they have to join in this time. I ask them to say and to show on their fingers the number they hear (*un, deux, trois*, etc), waving their hand in the air.

If you are a native French speaker or a language specialist, you know about '*la liaison*' (*deux* (z) *éléphants*, *trois* (z) *éléphants*), but I would suggest not mentioning this, as the pupils are yet too young to understand this concept.

Click on the link in the PPT (slide 29):
https://www.youtube.com/watch?v=ab9XaMTikwU

Extension B

This is a very simple but nice song with numbers up to 10. Ask the class to just listen to the song and watch the video once. Then play the song again and ask the pupils to listen first and then repeat. The song is great as it allows practising and singing in a very engaging way.

Click on the link in the PPT (slide 30):
https://www.youtube.com/watch?v=lsc3qLMaCu8

French is Fun at Key Stage 1

© Brilliant Publications Limited

4. How old are you?

Introduction

Let the class know that today they will be learning how to ask someone *Quel âge as-tu ?* (How old are you?) and how to answer this question. Ask the pupils what do they think they need to know if they would like to answer this question? Numbers, of course.

Learning objective

To ask someone how old they are and to answer in French.

Vocabulary

Quel âge as-tu ?	How old are you?
J'ai … an(s).	I am … years old
C'est quel numéro ?	What number is this?
À demain	See you tomorrow
À bientôt	See you soon

On the USB Drive

PPT presentation includes:
- question and answer (slides 3 and 14)
- ages without words (slides 4–13)
- ages with words (slides 15–24)

Additional resources needed

Flashcards from PPT
Small flashcards with pictures only (pages 71–72)
Small flashcards with words and pictures (pages 73–74)
Soft ball
Puppets
Numbers (plastic, magnetic or wooden)

Activities

1. Revise the numbers from 1 to 10 with the class. Clap your hands in different rhythms and patterns, calling out numbers and asking the class to repeat. Show the children a number on your fingers and ask *C'est quel numéro ?* Wait for them to answer.

2. Ask the pupils to sit in a circle around the carpet. Using a soft ball, the children pass the ball to the child next to them calling out the numbers in order. As a challenge, you can try this activity also counting down from 10 to 0.

3. Introduce the new question *Quel âge as-tu ?* I usually say that we can easily remember this question if we think that it sounds like a little sneeze at the end: *as-tu*. The children love this trick. After 'sneezing' a couple of times, practise the question word by word from the beginning. Use funny voices/ clapping hands or any other methods you have, but make sure you repeat the question many times, as it is quite difficult and hard to remember.

© Brilliant Publications Limited

French is Fun at Key Stage 1

4. When we teach this lesson to very young pupils, I explain that in French we don't say 'I am ... years old', but 'I have ... years old'. This is mainly because I am going to introduce *j'ai* in different contexts later in my lessons and I don't want them to get confused. However, my young pupils find this information funny and they will remember this fact.

5. Display slide 3 on the PPT, with the question/answer. Practise with different numbers, saying different ages. Put some plastic (or wooden/magnetic) numbers in a bag and ask the class to stand in two parallel lines, facing their partners. Ask one line to get a number each from your bag and the other line to ask *Quel âge as-tu ?*. Their partners must answer with *J'ai ...* (+ the number they have) *ans*. Then swap.

6. Get your puppets to have a couple of conversations in front of the class and ask each other *Quel âge as-tu ?* The pupils must listen carefully and at the end of each conversation they must say the puppets' age.

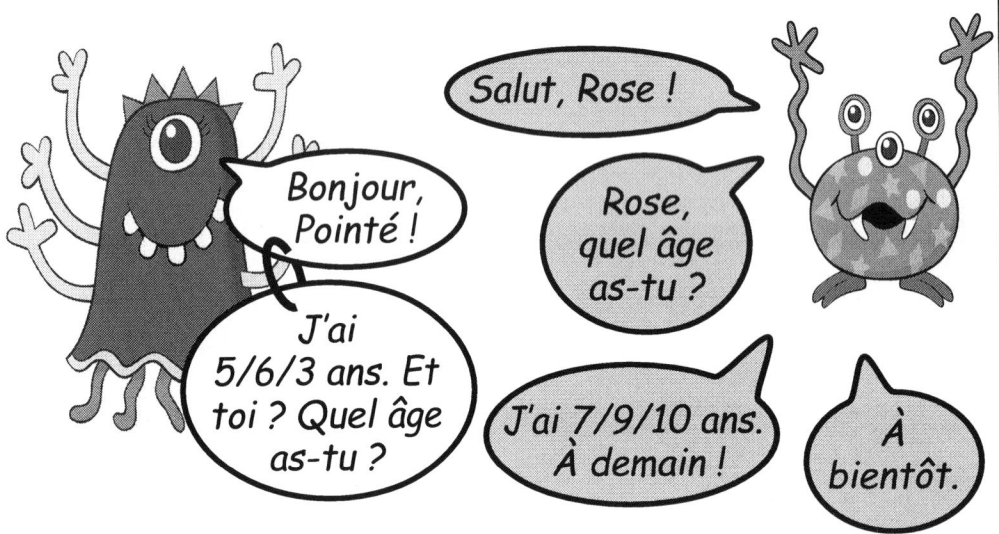

7. Practise saying *J'ai ... ans* with different ages using the PPT, first without words (slides 4–13) then with words (slides 15–24).

8. Ask the pupils to sit in a circle around the carpet. The teacher stands in the middle, with a soft ball. Pass the ball to a child and ask *Quel âge as-tu ?* The child must answer with *J'ai ... ans* and pass the ball back to you. After practising with the whole class, give the ball to a more confident child who will have to pass it to his/her partner, asking the target question. The partner must answer and ask the next child the same question, until everybody has had a go.

Extension

Introduce the new song, which is also a revision of some old topics. Ask the pupils to watch the video and listen to the song, then play the song again and ask the class to join in. As the song is in both English and French, it is very easy to understand. The pupils will be very tempted to talk about the pictures, but I always ask them to listen quietly, as they will hear two new numbers: 11 and 12, which we don't know yet.

Click on the link in the PPT (slide 25):
https://www.youtube.com/watch?v=NXkJ88ygPY0

French is Fun at Key Stage 1

5. Numbers 11 to 20

Introduction

Numbers are always such a great topic to teach as there are so many games and activities which you can do with them: from simple counting to challenging your class to count in twos or threes or even to working out some simple addition or subtraction.

Introduce the new lesson to the class. Let the pupils know that they will be revising today the numbers up to 10 and they will be learning the numbers up to 20.

After teaching the numbers to 20 you can now expand the counting down process to some other class activities. For example, 'You have 20 seconds to tidy up the room. I will count down from 20 to 0, by the time I reach 0, I expect you to be sitting quietly in your seat/at your table/ in your carpet space' or 'You have 20 seconds to put your PE bags away and return to the carpet, ready for the lesson, *vingt, dix-neuf, dix-huit ...* etc. Remember to praise the pupils as often as possible with *très bien !, super !, excellent !*

Learning objective
To learn the numbers 11 to 20 in French.

Vocabulary

onze	= 11	seize	= 16
douze	= 12	dix-sept	= 17
treize	= 13	dix-huit	= 18
quatorze	= 14	dix-neuf	= 19
quinze	= 15	vingt	= 20

On the USB Drive
PPT presentation includes:
- numbers 11–20 without words (slides 3–12)
- numbers 11–20 with words (slides 13–22)

Additional resources needed
Flashcards from the PPT (slides 3–22)
Small flashcards with pictures only (pages 75–76)
Small flashcards with words only (pages 77–78)
Numbers (plastic, magnetic or wooden)
Soft ball
Small whiteboards and whiteboard pens

Activities

1. Start your lesson revising numbers 0–10 using either flashcards (pages 65–70) or the PPT for lesson 3. Ask the class to count in English from 1 to 20, while you show the numbers on your cards.

2. Ask the children to work in small groups or with a partner, practising the numbers in French, from 1 to 10. When they finish, ask them to raise their hands and call out random numbers. After everybody has had a go, ask some more confident pupils to count now in order from 1 to 10.

3. Now introduce the numbers from 11–20, using the flashcards (pages 75–78) or the PPT presentation (slides 3–22). Call out each number many times, using various methods (funny voices, clap your hands in different rhythms and patterns). Ask the class to copy and repeat. Introduce the numbers first on their own and then with the spellings.

4. Give your pupils 5 or 10 seconds to make a circle on the carpet. Hand out for each child two plastic (or wooden/magnetic) numbers (one

onze

© Brilliant Publications Limited

French is Fun at Key Stage 1

17

of which should be 1) and ask them to put them together, so they will form a number from 10 to 20. The number should stay on the carpet, in front and facing each child. At this point, ask the children to look at the number they have, listen very quietly and carefully while you are counting from 10 to 20 and try to remember their number. After counting a few times using the flashcards and/or the PPT slides, go around to collect the numbers. Each child will call out the number they have.

5. Freeze the PPT on slide 23 with the numbers from 10 to 20 and play 'class vs teacher' (for the rules of the game, see page 13).

6. Play the 'tennis game'. The class is a team and they will play against you. Ask them to stand up. Use all the numbers from 1 to 20. Pretend you are holding an imaginary tennis racket and the ball is a number. You pass a number, the class passes back the next number: *un-deux; trois-quatre …* . When you finish, swap over, now the class starts: *un-deux; trois-quatre …* .

7. Give the children 5 minutes to play the 'tennis game' with a partner. They can also play this in threes. Quietly walk around, listening and helping those pupils who struggle.

8. Play a guessing game. Call out the numbers slowly a few times, allowing the pupils to remember all the numbers they have learnt today. Ask the children to choose one number from 10 to 20 and keep it secret from everybody. Invite a confident child to the front of the class and ask the rest of the class to guess the number they have chosen. The child who guesses the correct number takes their turn at the front of the class, and so on. I often play this game using 'the magic chair'. This is the teacher's chair and the children absolutely love to sit on it while playing this game!

9. Hold up a numbered flashcard and ask the class *C'est quel numéro ?* (What number is this?). The children must say the number in French.

10. Sit the pupils in a circle. Pass a soft ball from one to another, asking the class to count from 1 to 20. When they have finished, ask the class to return to their carpet / table spaces. An easy way to assess their progress at this point is thumbs up. 'Thumbs up if you can count from 1 to 12'; 'Thumbs up is you can count from 1 to 15', etc.

11. *Using the flashcards with numbers and spelling (pages 75–78) ask the pupils to work in small groups, at the table. Give each group two envelopes: one with numbers and one with spelling. Ask them to match the number with the correct spelling.

12. *Return to the carpet. Practise one more time all the numbers from 1 to 20 with the class. Give each child a small whiteboard and a whiteboard pen. Ask them to write on their whiteboard the number you call out in French and then show you their boards. Make sure your pupils understand they only have to write the numbers not the spellings.

douze

quinze

vingt

French is Fun at Key Stage 1

© Brilliant Publications Limited

I usually write some numbers on the whiteboard, just to avoid any confusion.

* These activities are a little advanced if you are teaching French to Reception children.

Extension

Talk to the class about the song they are going to listen to and practise. It covers numbers 1–20. Ask them to watch the video and listen to the song.

It's now time to stand up and join in! Show me the numbers on your fingers while singing.

Click on the link in the PPT (slide 24):

https://www.youtube.com/watch?v=UsEz58BbIMY

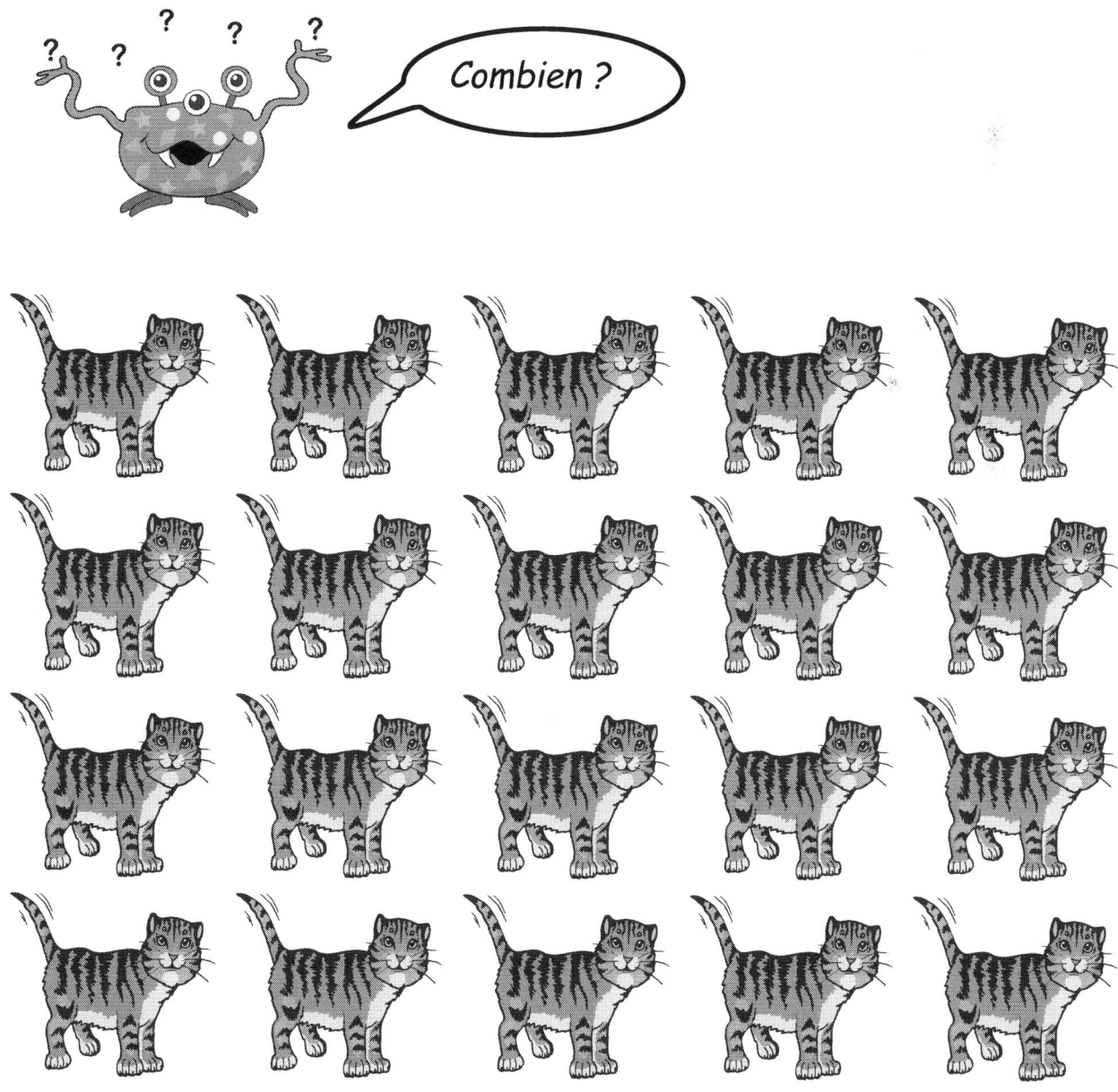

© Brilliant Publications Limited

French is Fun at Key Stage 1

19

6. Colours

Introduction

Talk to the class about which colours they know in English. Play with them 'Show me something (yellow)' and the pupils must touch that object in the class (or point at it, if that's easier for you). Explain to the pupils that some French colour words might sound or look very similar to the English ones, but remind them that the accent is slightly different, so they need to listen very carefully and pronounce the words exactly as they hear.

At the end of the lesson you can play this game again, but in French. Just replace "Show me ... " with *Montrez-moi ...* .

Learning objective
To learn the words for different colours in French.

Vocabulary

rouge	red
bleu	blue
jaune	yellow
vert	green
noir	black
blanc	white
orange	orange
violet	purple
rose	pink
marron	brown
gris	grey
C'est quelle couleur ?	Which colour is this?
Montrez-moi ...	Show me ...
Levez la main	Raise your hand
Levez-vous	Stand up
Asseyez-vous	Sit down
Quelle est ta couleur préférée ?	What is your favourite colour?

On the USB Drive
PPT presentation:
- pictures only (slides 3–13)
- pictures and words (slides 14–24)

Additional resources needed
Flashcards from the PPT (slides 3–24)
Small flashcards with pictures only (pages 79–80)
Small flashcards with words only (pages 81–82)
Small flashcards with words and pictures (pages 83–85)
Coloured pencils
Soft ball (multiple colours)
Puppets

Activities

1. Print out the individual slides on the PPT, both the ones with spelling and the ones without. Always start using the cards without the spelling. I usually go through all of the colours (slides 3–13) in English first, by asking the class to call out the colour they see on my card. Go through all the colours again using their French names. Practise a few

orange

French is Fun at Key Stage 1

© Brilliant Publications Limited

times so they become familiar before showing the children the spelling cards (slides 14–24). Try using different voices: loud voice, squeaky voice, weird voice, soft voice, funny voice, etc, for a fun activity.

2. Use the PPT to practise the colours one more time. Using a pot containing a variety of coloured pencils, choose a coloured pencil and ask the class to repeat the colour after you. Once you have practised a few times, hold up a coloured pencil and ask *C'est quelle couleur ?* After going through all the colours, put the pencils back in the pot. Ask a child to come to the front of the class and, without looking, choose a coloured pencil. Now they can open their eyes. She/he must answer the question *C'est quelle couleur ?* Invite other children to do the same. We always follow a rule when playing games: taking turns boy/girl, boy/girl or the other way around.

3. Freeze the PPT on slide 25 showing all the colours on it. Go through the colours a few times, pointing at them and asking the class to repeat. Invite two children to start the game. Ask them to stand in front of the board; explain that you will call out a colour by saying *Montrez-moi le couleur …* (+ colour) and the first child to touch the correct colour wins and will play against the next child. Allow every child in the class to have a go at this game. It is very funny, interactive and it gives you the chance to repeat the target vocabulary without the children noticing.

4. Ask the children to sit in small groups on the carpet (4/5 children per group) and hand each group two sets of flashcards: one showing the colours only and the other the spellings. Give the groups 5 minutes to match the colour with the correct spelling. To finish ask them to call out, in a group, what colours they have.

5. If your class uses a carpet with different coloured squares (usually each square on the carpet is a pupil's space), this is another funny activity for the lesson. Ask the pupils to stand up when they hear the colour they are sitting on: *Rouge, levez-vous !* ; *Vert, levez-vous ! Orange, levez-vous !* etc. When everybody is up, do the same in reverse. This time, the children will need to sit down: *Bleu, asseyez-vous ! Violet, asseyez-vous !* etc. Before giving instructions or asking short questions in French, I will say 'Now, I am going to ask you to sit down/ stand up/ put your hand up in French. So when I say … it means … . Never doubt the pupils' ability to follow your instructions or to answer your French questions. Just use plenty of actions to help them understand what you say (for example, raise your hand when you say *levez la main !* or put your finger to your lips for *silence !*).

6. Freeze the PPT on slide 25 with all the colours and play 'class versus teacher' (see page 13). We usually play the game three times and only sometimes, as a reward for great behaviour, will play the fourth round.

7. Make a circle and ask the class to pass the ball around and say a different colour. When they finish, ask the children to pass the ball around once again. This time, they have to say and point at a colour which is on the ball. Return to the carpet spaces.

rouge

rose

vert

blanc

bleu

© Brilliant Publications Limited

French is Fun at Key Stage 1

8. Using the PPT presentation, practise all the colours again with the class. Show a colour to the class and ask *C'est quelle couleur ?*

   Use your puppets to have a short conversation about their favourite colours: *Quelle est ta couleur préférée ?* (What is your favourite colour?) *Ma couleur préférée c'est le …* (My favourite colour is …).

marron

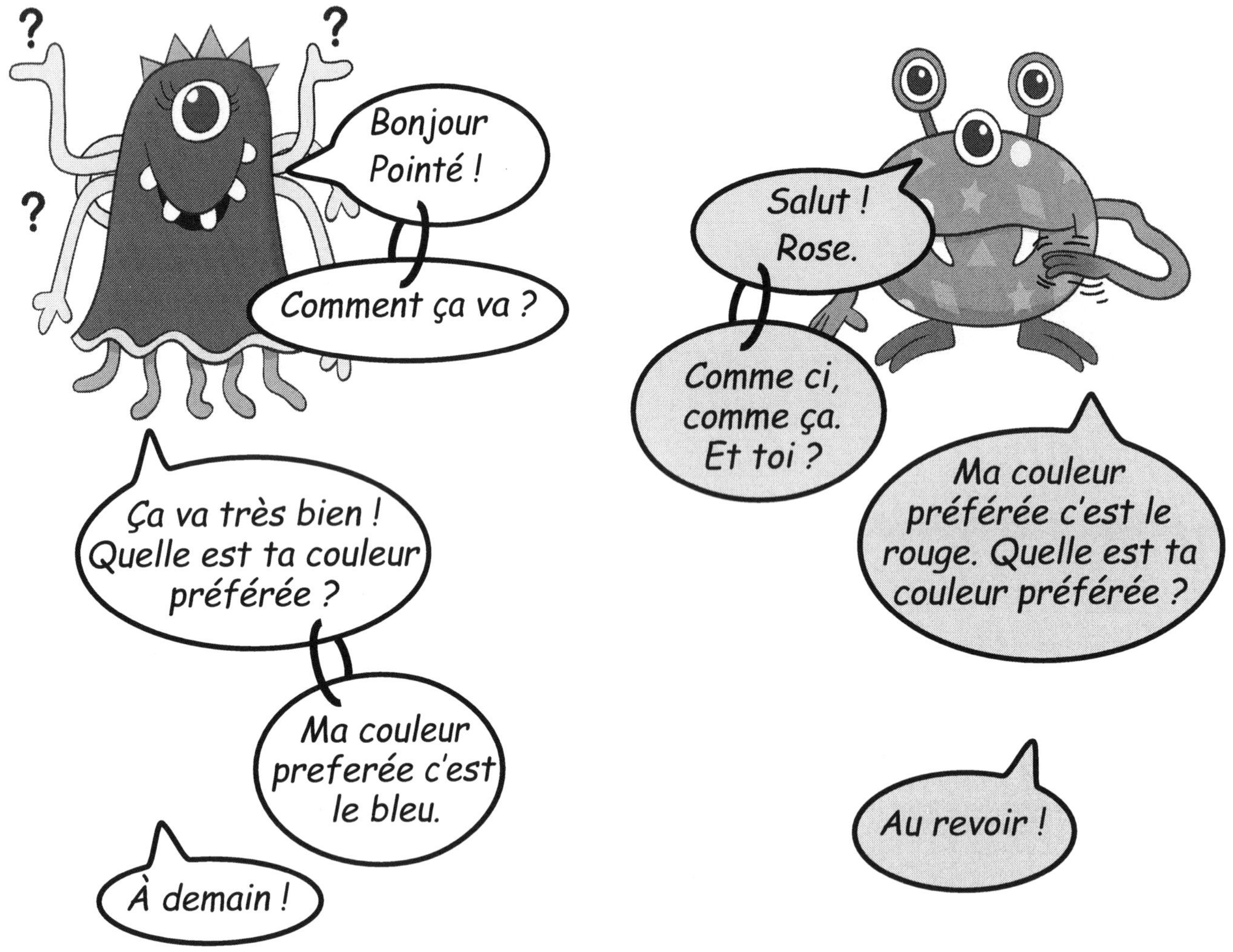

Bonjour Pointé !

Comment ça va ?

Salut ! Rose.

Comme ci, comme ça. Et toi ?

Ça va très bien ! Quelle est ta couleur préférée ?

Ma couleur préférée c'est le rouge. Quelle est ta couleur préférée ?

Ma couleur preferée c'est le bleu.

Au revoir !

À demain !

9. Now the puppets will ask each child *Quelle est ta couleur préférée ?* You can either invite the children to come to the front of the class and talk to the puppets or they can sit in a circle while you move around. At this point, just ask them to say the colour only, rather than the whole sentence. However, if you teach this lesson in Year 2 you could use the PPT slide 26 with the question and the answer and encourage your pupils to answer now in a sentence. Have a vote on which is the class's favourite colour.

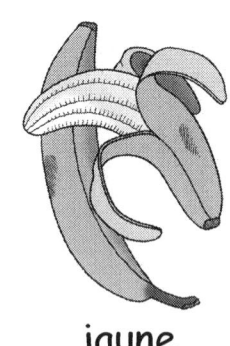
jaune

French is Fun at Key Stage 1

© Brilliant Publications Limited

22

Extension A

Talk to the class about the song they are going to listen to and practise. Invite them to watch the video and listen to the song and ask if they recognised the tune. Of course, they did! Now it is time to stand up, do the same actions as for the 'Head, shoulders, knees and toes', but with the French lyrics. Trust me, it is funny if you have a go too!

Click on the link in the PPT (slide 27):
https://www.youtube.com/watch?v=zduapTwsSwA

Extension B

Freeze the PPT on slide 28. Hand out different small coloured cards and ask the pupils to come to the front, two or three at a time, to stick their card in the correct place using Blu Tack®. When they finish, check if the cards are matched correctly with the colours.

7. Days of the week

Introduction

Talk to the class about what they will be learning today. Ask the pupils to recite the days of the week in English.

Talk to the children about planets (and other celestial objects), showing them the pictures on the cards (see PPT slides 3–9). At this stage, just talk about the English names for the planets and don't click on the audio links which give the days of the week in French.

Any facts you could share about each planet would be great and you will be surprised how many things the children know already. Mention that the Sun is a star not a planet. Most of the children will probably already know this.

Explain that it will be easier to remember the days of the week in French if they think of the names of the planets, but of course some things in space have a different name in French, the Moon/*la lune* and the Sun/*le soleil*.

Learning objective
To learn the days of the week in French.

Vocabulary

lundi	Monday
la lune	the Moon
mardi	Tuesday
mercredi	Wednesday
jeudi	Thursday
vendredi	Friday
samedi	Saturday
dimanche	Sunday
le soleil	the Sun

On the USB Drive

PPT presentation includes:
- planets with pictures only (slides 3–9)
- days of the week with words and pictures (slides 10–16)

Additional resources needed

Flashcards from the PPT (slides 10–16)
Small flashcards with words only (page 86)
Small flashcards with words divided (page 87)
Soft ball
Small bags/ little boxes

Activities

1. After introducing the new lesson and talking with the class about the planets, ask the children if they remember how to count to 10 in French. Choose some confident pupils to count up to 10 and play a quick tennis game with the class (you say a number, the class says the next one). As a challenge, you might ask them to guess why they need numbers when learning the days of the week. Of course, because there are seven days in a week, clever class! Let the class know that you will be using the numbers to 7 in your lesson in different activities.

2. Practise the days of the week (listen and repeat) using PPT slides 3–9. Explain that the French names for the days of the week are related to the names of the planet *Mars = mardi*, *Mercury = mercredi* etc. The exceptions are *lundi* (Monday; *la lune* = the Moon) and *dimanche* (Sunday). The top audio link gives the French name of the planet (or other celestial object). The bottom audio link gives the French name for the related day of the week.

lundi
(la lune)

French is Fun at Key Stage 1

© Brilliant Publications Limited

3. Now introduce the days of the week with the spelling (PPT slides 10–16) and explain some pronunciation rules (for example *lundi* – nasal pronunciation). When I have to model a nasal pronunciation, we usually play with this by asking the children to hold their nose and say the word, then try to sound that word exactly the same, but without holding their nose. At this stage, do not insist much on spelling but make sure you let the pupils know that, as they have probably already noticed, in French we do not write the days of the week with capital letters (with one important exception: if they are at the start of the sentence, we must use a capital letter).

4. Use a variety of voices, clapping hands, rhythms, etc, to practise each day of the week: *lun-di* (clap-clap); *mar-di* (clap-clap); *mer-cre-di* (clap-clap-clap). Ask the class if they can say *lundi* with a quiet voice? Can you say *mardi* with a squeaky voice? Can you say *mercredi* with a loud voice? And so on. The pupils love using voices while practising.

5. Ask the class to stand up and copy you. Put your hands up, using your fingers for each day of the week and practise the days in order, from *lundi* to *dimanche*. Now ask the class just to say *di* when you say the beginning of the word, and they have to add the *di* at the end. Remind them that *dimanche* starts with *di*, so they have to be very careful when it is their turn to start. Practise a couple of times, saying the days in order from *lundi* to *dimanche* and from *dimanche* to *lundi*. Explain to them that *di* means day. Challenge: swap around. Now you say *di* and the class have to call out the rest of the word.

6. Ask the class to sit in a circle and give them a soft ball. They have to pass the ball to the person who sits next to them and say a day of the week they remember, in random order. I usually stand in the middle of the circle and call out the days of the week a couple of times (listen and repeat) before I give them the ball. Repeat this activity, but now ask the class to pass the ball around and say the days of the week in order.

7. Pupils sit in small groups of 3–4 on the carpet or at tables. Give them a small bag/ a little box containing the laminated flashcards with words (page 87) and ask them to put the two parts together so they can make a day. Show them an example: *lun + di = lundi*. As an extension,

mardi
(Mars)

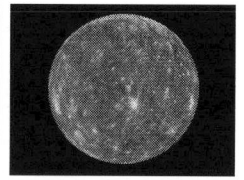

mercredi
(Mercure)

jeudi
(Jupiter)

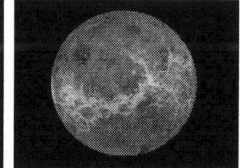

vendredi
(Vénus)

© Brilliant Publications Limited

French is Fun at Key Stage 1

you can ask them to put the days in order, after they have finished the previous activity.

8. Play a guessing game. Ask the children to choose one day of the week and keep it secret. Invite a more confident child to come to the front of the class to start the game, then ask the rest of the children if they can guess which day the other child has chosen.

9. Call out the days of the week in order starting at *lundi*, and use your fingers to show which day is that: 1: *lundi*, 2: *mardi*, 3: *mercredi*, etc. After practising with the class a few times, now show a number on your fingers and ask *C'est quel jour le jour numéro ... un, deux, trois ... sept ?* The pupils must answer with the correct day.

10. Show the flashcards with spelling (page 86) and practise the days again. Ask the pupils to *Levez la main, s'il vous plait ...* if they can tell you a day which starts with '**v**'/ a day which starts with '**d**'/ a day which starts with '**j**'.

11. Play a tennis game. Ask the class to stand up. Pretend you are holding an imaginary tennis racket and the ball is a day of the week. You pass a day, the class passes back the ball saying the next day: *lundi-mardi; mercredi-jeudi; vendredi-samedi; dimanche*. When you finish, swap around. Now the class starts: *lundi-mardi; mercredi-jeudi*, etc. Give the children 5 minutes to play the tennis game with a partner, while you are walking around, listening and ready to support or model the pronunciation.

12. Chinese whispers. The children absolutely love playing Chinese whispers. The class will sit in a circle. Choose one child to whisper a day of the week to the child sitting next to him/her. The last person must say the word out loud. If this is the correct word, they can play the game one more time.

13. Write vertically on the whiteboard the numbers from 1 to 7. Using the big flashcards with spelling, ask the class to help you put the days in order. Show a card and ask *Jeudi, c'est quel numéro ? Dimanche, c'est quel numéro ? Lundi, c'est quel numéro ?* etc. The pupils must call out the number in French and the teacher will stick the card next to the correct number.

samedi (Saturne)

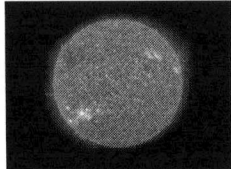

dimanche (le soleil)

Extension

Talk to the class about the song they are going to listen to. Explain that this is a song about a little prince (petit prince) who goes together with his dad (le roi = the king) and mum (la reine = the queen) to visit a little boy. But the boy is not at home, so they will return the next day, and the next day and so on.

Before you start the song, let the pupils know that they have a very important task to complete: there is one day missing in our song. If they know which one, at the end of the song they will have to raise their hand. Click on the link in the PPT (slide 17):

https://www.youtube.com/watch?v=noo1_wUGsIU

French is Fun at Key Stage 1

© Brilliant Publications Limited

8. Animals and pets

Introduction

Teaching the names of the animals is always one of the best lessons of the school year. Most of the children have a pet at home and all of them love animals, so the lesson will be very funny and engaging. Hide plastic or material animals around the classroom: under the tables, chairs, behind some books, on the pegs, etc, before the lesson starts. Believe me, it's going to be great fun for the children to try finding them at the end of the lesson.

Learning objective
To learn the names for some animals and pets in French.

Vocabulary

un chat	a cat
un chien	a dog
un lapin	a rabbit
un oiseau	a bird
un serpent	a snake
une tortue	a turtle
une souris	a mouse
un cochon d'Inde	a Guinea pig
un poisson	a fish
une araignée	a spider

On the USB Drive

PPT presentation includes:
- animals with pictures only (slides 3–12)
- animals with words and pictures (slides 13–22)

Additional resources needed

Flashcards from the PPT
Small flashcards with pictures only (one for each child) (pages 88–90)
Small flashcards with words and pictures (pages 91–93)
Plastic/ fabric toy animals
Soft ball
Small bag/ box

Activities

1. After greeting the class, introduce the new lesson. (I usually start by asking them if they have pets at home and which is their favourite animal.) After the pupils have answered, show them the slides on the PPT (slides 3–12) and firstly, ask them to name the animals in English.

2. Go through the animals and decide with your class which actions or mimes would best represent each animal. The children are amazing at this and they always have such great ideas!

3. Introduce the French name of the animals now, using the PPT (slides 3–12) or the flashcards without words (pages 88–90) initially and the action for each animal. After the class has practised a few times, show them the flashcards with spelling and remind the pupils that, as

un cochon d'Inde

un poisson

© Brilliant Publications Limited

French is Fun at Key Stage 1

they are aware by now, there is going to be a difference between the spelling and the pronunciation. If this lesson is taught in Year 1 or Year 2, you can point attention to '**ch**' being pronounced 'sh' or to 'h' being silent at the beginning of the word '(h)amster'. Practise as many times as possible, modelling the pronunciation and using the flashcards/ PPT slides/ actions.

4. Ask the class to now listen one more time to the names of the animals they have learnt today, paying attention to each action/ mime you have decided to use. When you finish, call out a name of an animal and ask the class to show you the action for this animal. *Montrez-moi …* (show me …)

5. Give the class 5 or 10 seconds to make a circle on the carpet, while you are counting down. Standing in the middle of the circle and moving around so all the pupils can see you, call out again the names of the animals and ask the pupils to repeat after you and to remember as many names as possible. Passing the soft ball from one to another, the children must call out a name of an animal they remember.

6. Count down from 10 to 0 while pupils return to their carpet/home spaces. Let the class know that you have a very exciting mission for them. They need to find the animals you have hidden around the class. Send just 3–4 pupils at a time to look for an animal. If they find it, they must bring this to you. Give instructions in French, by explaining what you have asked for: *Trouvez un chat/ un chien/ un hamste*r, (find me a cat/dog/hamster) etc. Once they have found all the animals, put them in the magic bag and return to the carpet.

7. Freeze the PPT on slide 23 which depicts all the animals. Call out again their names with *écoutez et répétez*, then call out different animals and ask the children to come to the front and touch the correct picture: *Montrez moi …*

8. Keep the pictures on the board and play 'Class versus teacher' (see page 13).

9. Ask the pupils to choose one animal and remember the action for that animal. Invite one pupil at a time to the front of the class to show the action and choose someone to guess the name of the animal. The pupil who says the correct name comes to the front next.

10. Give each child one of the flashcard animal pictures (pages 88–90). Ask them to remember which animal is on their picture by practising one more time the animal names. Let the class know that you will call out an animal in French. If they have that picture, they need to stand up. 'Stand up if you have *un chat*. Stand up if you have *un chien, un lapin*', etc. When all the children are standing, ask them now to sit down if they hold a card with the animal you call out: 'Sit down if you have *un hamster*, sit down if you have *un oiseau*', etc.

un serpent

un chien

une souris

un chat

un lapin

une araignée

French is Fun at Key Stage 1

© Brilliant Publications Limited

11. The children must keep their cards and make a circle now. Get a small bag and go around to collect the pictures while asking *C'est quel animal ?* (Which animal is this?) The pupils say the name of the animal and then place the card in your bag. Of course, you are there to help them if they don't remember the name of the animal!

un oiseau

12. Ask the class to raise their hands in they remember the names of two/ three/ four, and then five animals in French. It is a very simple way to assess the pupils.

une tortue

Extension

At the end of the lesson you could read a beautiful story in French – 'Do you want to be my friend?' You might like to revise quickly the days of the week beforehand. This is a lesson I have created and it can be downloaded for free on the TES website.

Click on the link in the PPT (slide 24):

https://www.tes.com/teaching-resource/la-souris-qui-cherchait-un-ami-days-of-the-week-11680172

It has very nice pictures, and pupils absolutely love this story. If you read this, add in some actions and point to the pictures, I can guarantee this will be a great success. Such a nice way to finish this lesson!

Bonne chance !

© Brilliant Publications Limited

French is Fun at Key Stage 1

9. Fruit

Introduction

Greet the class and ask them *Comment ça va ?* We usually use thumbs up or down when I say 'Who is today … *ça va bien ?*' 'Who is today…*ça va mal ?*' etc. Of course, the pupils love to hear me saying *désolée*, if they are *ça va mal !* or *ça va très mal !*

Let the children know that today they will learn the names of some fruit and that, by the end of the lesson, you hope they will be able to say which fruit they like or they dislike.

Learning objectives

To learn the names of some fruit and to say which fruits you like or dislike in French.

Vocabulary

une/la banane	a/the banana
une/la pomme	a/the apple
une/l'orange	an/the orange
un/l'ananas	a/the pineapple
une/la pêche	a/the peach
une/la poire	a/the pear
une/la fraise	a/the strawberry
une/la cerise	a/the cherry
les …	the … (plural)
Aimes-tu … ?	Do you like…?
J'aime …	I like…
Je n'aime pas …	I don't like…
J'adore …	I love…
Je déteste …	I don't like at all…

On the USB Drive

PPT presentation includes:
- fruit with pictures only (slides 3–10)
- fruit with words and pictures (slides 11–18)
- likes and dislikes (slide 20)

Additional resources needed

Small flashcards of fruit with pictures only (pages 94–95)
Small flashcards of fruit with words and pictures (pages 96–97)
Plastic/ fabric fruit
Puppets
Soft ball
Small bag/ box

Note

When asking in French, "Do you like … + the name of the fruit?", you need to use the definite article in the plural form: *les* (the):
Aimes-tu les bananes ?/ Aimes-tu les oranges ?
If you plan to teach the song in the Extension, consider using the definite article *le/la/l'* rather than the indefinite article *un/une*.

Depending on your class's level of understanding, you can explain the difference between *un/une* and *le/la/l'/les*. Starting with Year 2, I would suggest introducing the genders of nouns gradually, by making pupils aware of the difference between English and French, or the difference between '*un*', '*une*', or '*le*' and '*la*', etc.

French is Fun at Key Stage 1

© Brilliant Publications Limited

Activities

1. Using slides 3–10 on the PPT or the flashcards with pictures only (pages 94–95), ask the class to say (in English for the moment) which fruit is on each card. Start practising now *écoutez et répétez !* (listen and repeat) the French names. After a few good practices, introduce the flashcards with words and pictures (pages 96–97) or slides 11–18 on the PPT. Remind the pupils that they need to repeat exactly what they hear, even if the word is spelt the same as in English, for example, 'orange'.

2. Show the slides of the PPT and practise the new vocabulary one more time. Just to make this *écoutez et répétez !* (listen and repeat) part of the lesson less obvious, use different ways to practise. Alternate clapping hands for example, *une o–range/ un a-na-nas*, etc. By using funny voices, you can say *une pomme* with a squeaky voice, *une poire* with a quiet voice and *une fraise* with a loud voice.

3. Ask the class to make a circle around the carpet in *cinq, quatre, trois* … . Practise the vocabulary together one more time then give the soft ball to a more confident child who needs to say the name of a fruit and pass the ball to the next child. When they finish, ask them to remain in the circle.

4. Making sure that all the pupils can see you, show them the fruit you have in your bag: *C'est une banane, une poire, une pomme.* Put the fruit back and let the class know that you will now be walking outside the circle and you will put a fruit behind each child. They can touch and feel the fruit, but they are not allowed to look. The pupils must guess the name of the fruit they touch. Once they have made their guess show them the fruit to verify if they were right.

5. Play a guessing game: Place a set of flashcards face down and invite each child to take a card but not to look at the picture. Ask them *C'est quel fruit ?* (What fruit is this?) Each pupil then tries to guess the fruit. Then show the card to the rest of the class and ask *C'est un/une … ?* plus the fruit the pupils said. The rest of the class should say *Oui.* if they are right, or *Non.* if they are wrong.

6. Hand out the small flashcards, one for each child. Ask the pupils to hold their cards up when they hear the name of the fruit on their card: *Montrez-moi une pomme/une orange/un ananas* (Show me an apple…). When you finish, ask the children to swap cards with the person sitting next to them. Repeat the activity. Using a small bag/box walk around and collect the cards asking each child *C'est quel fruit ?*

7. Freeze the PPT on slide 19 showing all the fruit. Go through the names of the fruit again. Point to each one as you go and ask the class to repeat. Divide the children into pairs. Then choose one pair to start the game. Invite them to stand in front of the IWB, you call out a fruit by saying *Montrez-moi le … .* The first child who touches the correct fruit will get a point. Try to let every pair have a go.

une/la banane

une/l' orange

un/l' ananas

une/la pêche

une/la poire

© Brilliant Publications Limited

French is Fun at Key Stage 1

8. At this point, the pupils should be able to remember most of the fruit they have learnt. It is now time to introduce 'likes and dislikes'. My suggestion would be to introduce all the phrases, but for this lesson only use *J'aime ...* and *Je n'aime pas ...* . The other two could be introduced in the next lesson, when you can revise the fruit and practise more likes/dislikes. After explaining what *aimes-tu ... ?* (do you like ...?) means, practise different answers with the class.

9. Using your 'talking puppets' start a conversation letting the class know that the puppets will be asking each other which fruit they like, or what they don't like. When the puppets have finished their conversation, the children should say which fruit each puppet likes/doesn't like.

une/la fraise

10. Now it is the children's turn to answer the question *Aimes-tu ... ?* Holding up the coloured picture only flashcards, ask the pupils: *Aimes-tu les pommes / les bananes / les fraises ?* etc. The pupils answer raising their hands up.

une/la cerise

French is Fun at Key Stage 1

If you decide to stop here and teach the song in the next lesson, then you can finish this lesson with a very simple activity: a guessing game. Think of a fruit and the children have to guess which one it is.

une/la pomme

Extension

Talk to the class about the song they will listen to and the video they will watch. Explain the song is called *J'aime les fruits* and ask what they think it means: 'I like fruit!'

Click on the link in the PPT (slide 21):

https://www.youtube.com/watch?v=nJ03KjwiIVM

The pupils will watch and listen first. Play the song one more time and ask the class to join in. They need to make a circle around the carpet, hands on the shoulders of the person in front. The teacher will lead the 'dance' by holding one child's hand and you will finish the lesson with great samba moves and lots of laughter. Encourage the class to sing '*J'aime les fruit*' alongside dancing.

We normally make any adult in the school who passes by our class watch us. Sometimes, they will even join in with the rest of the class.

10. Months of the year

Introduction

Talk to the class about the new lesson and ask the children to say the month they were born in. Let them know that you hope each child will be able to say this month in French by the end of the lesson. Challenge the class to call out the months in order, from January to December.

Tip: often displayed in KS1 classrooms there will be days of the week, numbers, colours and months etc. Take every opportunity to use them in your French lessons. For example, when you challenge the class to say the months in order, point at the chart and encourage every child to join in. Ask them how many months are in a year and count them in French.

Learning objective

To learn the names of the months of the year in French.

Vocabulary

janvier	January
février	February
mars	March
avril	April
mai	May
juin	June
juillet	July
août	August
septembre	September
octobre	October
novembre	November
décembre	December

On the USB Drive

PPT presentation includes:
- months with pictures only (slides 3–14)
- months with words and pictures (slides 15–26)

Additional resources needed

Flashcards from the PPT (slides 3–26)
Small flashcards with words only (page 98)
Puppets
Soft ball

Activities

1. Using the PPT with pictures only initially (slides 3–14), introduce the French months, asking the class to *écoutez et répétez !* (listen and repeat). Do this again, but now use the slides with words and pictures (slides 15–26). As usual, remind the pupils that they need to listen carefully to your pronunciation first and next they have to repeat. When you have practised a couple of times, try to say three months at a time, then ask the class to repeat: *Écoutez, janvier, février, mars et répétez, janvier, février, mars*, etc. Clapping hands now *jan-vi-er, fé-vri-er, mars, a-vril, mai, ju-in … .*

2. Ask the pupils to raise their hands up and wriggle their fingers. Remind them that at the beginning of the lesson they have counted to 12 because there are 12 months in a year. Count together from 1 to 12. Now let's say the months in order from *janvier* to *décembre*, by showing also on our fingers which number that month is.

janvier

février

French is Fun at Key Stage 1

3. Invite the class to stand up and put their hands together, ready for a clap. Let the children know that this will be a challenge, as we will try to say the months in order from *janvier* to *décembre* and then backwards. Always model this type of activity. Hands together, the teacher and the pupils will crouch down, touching the carpet with the tips of their fingers. This is the starting point. Clap once *janvier, répétez !* Clap again: *février, répétez !*, etc. With each clap we raise hands a bit, so by the time the class says *décembre* the hands are up in the air above their heads. Now go backwords, making sure you leave enough space between each clap, so by the time the children repeat *janvier* they are touching the floor again with the tips of their fingers. Now they can sit down and listen to you calling out the months one more time, using visual support (PPT).

4. Freeze the board on slide 27 of the provided PPT. The class call out the months in blue and you, the teacher, the months in red. Swap over: the class will now call out the months in red and the teacher, the months in blue. Working with a partner, the children will repeat this activity while you walk around listening, ready to give support. Remember to swap over!

5. The pupils make a circle around the carpet. Repeat the months and ask the children to remember how to say in French the month when they celebrate their birthday. They need to pass around the soft ball and say that month. When everybody has had a go, return to the home spaces.

6. The teacher will call out a month in French and the pupils will say which month that is in English. *Janvier: C'est quel mois ?* (January). *Juillet: C'est quel mois ?* (July). *Septembre: C'est quel mois ?* (September), etc.

7. Make a circle around the carpet. This time challenge the class to say the months in order from *janvier* to *décembre* while passing the soft ball from one child to another. Always stay in the middle of the circle, ready to support the pupils who struggle or need a bit of extra help.

8. Divide the class in small groups of 4–5 children. Using the flashcard of slide 28, hand out one per group also giving them the small flashcards with spelling. Each group must stick the correct French word on the pictures (provide some adhesive putty or sticky tape). Give them 5–7 minutes then walk around and check the answers.

9. Hold a flashcard with no spelling in the air and ask the class *C'est quel mois ?* The pupils must answer in French.

10. Tell me a month which starts with … a, j, d, m, etc.

11. Stand up/sit down game. This is always an activity the children love to play. Ask them to stand up when they hear the month that their birthday is in. When everybody is standing, ask the class to sit down when they hear the same month.

mars

avril

mai

juin

juillet

août

© Brilliant Publications Limited

French is Fun at Key Stage 1

12. Play a guessing game. Go through the months again several times until the children are familiar with them. Ask each pupil to choose a month and to keep it a secret from each other. Ask one pupil to come to the front of the class while the rest of the pupils try to guess. Alternate between boy/girl until all pupils have had a turn.

13. Using the puppets to assist you, play the 'tennis game' (see page 18), saying the months in order. At this point, encourage the pupils to join in as your puppets might struggle a bit playing this game. *Trois, deux, un … . Start.*

14. Ask the children to close their eyes a minute, while they listen to you calling out the months. They must try to remember how to say in French the month of their birthday. Open your eyes now and answer my question *C'est quand ton anniversaire ?* (When is your birthday?).

septembre

octobre

novembre

décembre

Extension A

Let the children know that they are going to listen to a very nice song about the months, but they have a task: while watching the video and listening to the song, they have to put their hands up (and down) every time they hear the month of their birthday. Alternatively, they can stand up/sit down if they are at the tables/on chairs. As children get easily over-excited during this type of activity, we always have a rule: extra marbles/stickers/points, etc if we are very sensible.

Click on the link in the PPT (slide 29):

https://www.youtube.com/watch?v=KUqVhf9oUqQ

French is Fun at Key Stage 1 © Brilliant Publications Limited

Extension B

A second song that the pupils can listen to (they can join in with the months, while playing the song one more time). The teacher can explain that the song is about an old gentleman, *Monsieur le Temps* (Mr Time), who is going to the market to buy twelve months for a calendar from *Madame L'Année* (Mrs Year)

Click on the link in the PPT (slide 30):

https://www.youtube.com/watch?v=2odJakoOVVI

11. Parts of the body

Introduction

Ask the class if they know the song 'Head, shoulders, knees and toes'. Of course, they do! Sing the song together, using the actions. Let the pupils know that today they will learn the body parts and that, by the end of the lesson they will be able to sing this song in French.

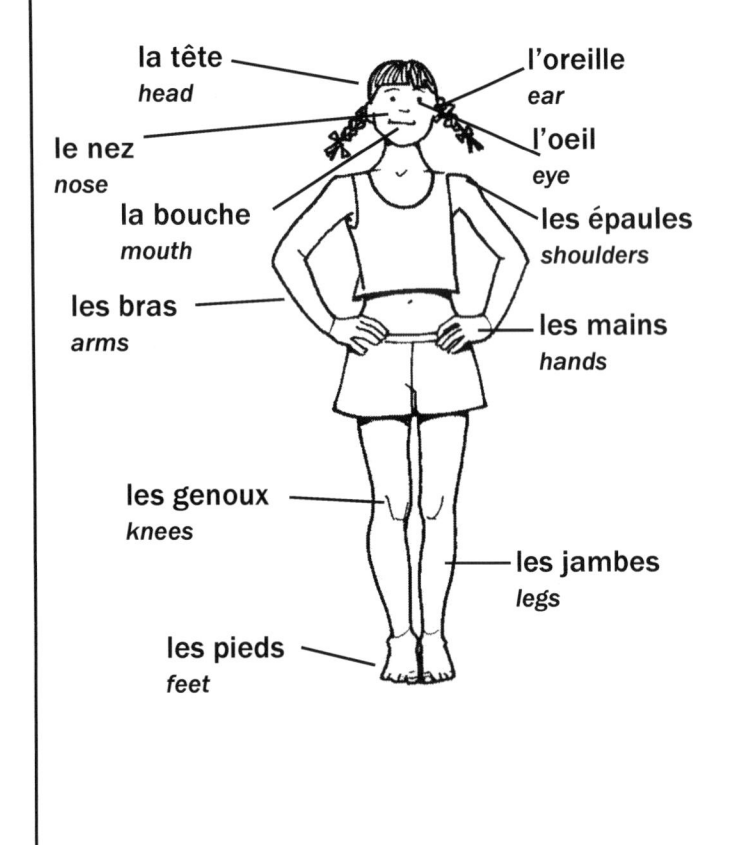

- la tête – head
- l'oreille – ear
- l'oeil – eye
- le nez – nose
- la bouche – mouth
- les épaules – shoulders
- les bras – arms
- les mains – hands
- les genoux – knees
- les jambes – legs
- les pieds – feet

Learning objective

To learn the names for different parts of the body in French.

Vocabulary

la tête	the head
l'épaule / les épaules	the shoulder(s)
le genou / les genoux	the knee(s)
le pied / les pieds	the foot/feet
l'oeil / les yeux	the eye(s)
l'oreille / les oreilles	the ear(s)
la bouche	the mouth
le nez	the nose
Où est … ?	Where is…?
Où sont … ?	Where are…?
Touchez …	Touch…
Montrez-moi …	Show me…
J'ai mal à la/l'/ au/aux …	My … hurt(s)
un bec	a beak

On the USB Drive

PPT presentation includes:
- parts of the body with pictures only (slides 3–10)
- parts of the body with words and pictures (slides 11–18)

Additional resources needed

Flashcards from the PPT (slides 3–18)
Small flashcards pictures of different parts of the body (pages 99–100)
Plaster cards (page 100: one plaster per team)
Puppets
Adhesive putty

Activities

1. Show the class the slides on the PPT with pictures only (slides 3–10) or big flashcards and ask which part of the body is in the picture. Make sure the cards are in the song order: head, shoulders, knees, feet (toes), eyes, ear, mouth and nose, and practise them in this order for the whole lesson. This will help children memorise the song easily at the end of the lesson.

2. Call out the body parts in French, using PPT (slides 3–10) or the big flashcards with pictures only initially. When practising 'pieds' explain that the French song is a slightly different version to the English, in that

la tête

French is Fun at Key Stage 1

© Brilliant Publications Limited

they use 'feet' in their song instead of toes. Introduce the spellings now and remind the pupils to repeat exactly what they hear.

3. Ask the pupils to stand up, repeat and touch that part of the body. Always model this type of activity: *la tête, les épaules, les genoux*, etc.

4. Show the flashcards of the different parts of the body and ask the class to watch and listen carefully. Call out each part of the body a few times. Alternate showing the class the pictures and pointing at/ touching that part of your body. Ask the pupils to touch the correct part of the body when you say *Touchez* (touch) *le nez, les oreilles, les genoux*, etc.

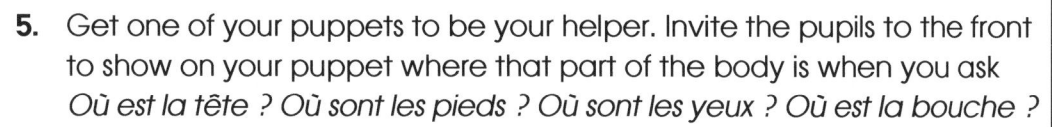

5. Get one of your puppets to be your helper. Invite the pupils to the front to show on your puppet where that part of the body is when you ask *Où est la tête ? Où sont les pieds ? Où sont les yeux ? Où est la bouche ?*

6. Using the PPT presentation, call out the body parts again and ask the class to repeat. It is time to introduce the song. The pupils will stand up and will repeat after the teacher, touching the correct part of the body. Remember to do this in the same order as in the song.

7. If you have a good voice, sing the French song for the class. After they have listened to the song, ask the pupils to stand up and join in with actions and singing.

   Alternatively, click on the link on slide 21 of the PPT to help you:

   https://www.youtube.com/watch?v=pgXXTWKjk-Q

8. Play a 'Simon says' game – *Jacques a dit*. The pupils need to stand up. The teacher says *Jacques a dit touchez le nez/les yeux/les genoux*, etc. If they touch the wrong part of the body, they have to sit down.

9. Chinese whispers – one of the games the pupils will always ask you to play in your lesson. Sit the pupils in a circle, trying to have two more confident students next to each other: one to start the game and one to finish, calling out loud that part of the body. Show them again the flashcards/ PPT slides and ask the child starting the game to choose one word that he/she will whisper to the person sitting next to them. The last child in the circle will call out loud that word. If it is the correct

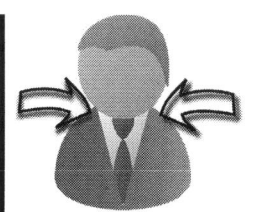

les épaules

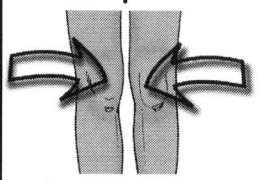

les genoux

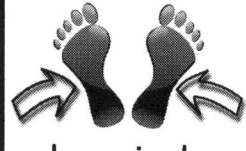

les pieds

les yeux

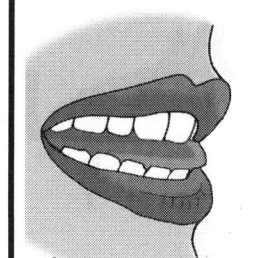

la bouche

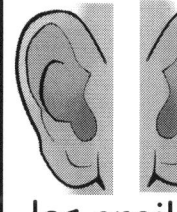

les oreilles

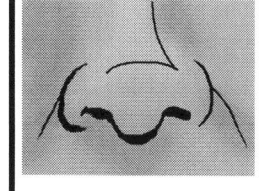

le nez

© Brilliant Publications Limited

French is Fun at Key Stage 1

one, they can play one more time (choose two different children to start and finish the game).

10. After returning to their carpet/ home spaces, practise the names for the parts of the body again using either the flashcards or the PPT presentation. Freeze on slide 19 and explain that the boy in the picture needs 'help'. Divide the class in small teams of 4–5 pupils. Hand out the flashcards of the plaster (page 100) explaining that *j'ai mal* means it hurts. When the teacher says *J'ai mal à la … / à l'… / au …/ aux …* (+ a part on the body), the teams will have 10 seconds to discuss which part on the body that is. One person in each team must come to the front of the class and stick the plaster (using adhesive putty) on the correct part of the body.

11. Cards above the head game. Invite a more confident child to come to the front of the class to start the game. Bring a chair, so he/she can sit down. The teacher holds a card (use the flashcards without spelling) above the child's head and asks three times. *C'est quoi ?* (What is this?) Without looking, the child will try to guess the part of the body which is in the picture. The rest of the class can help only by saying *oui*, if the pupil guessing is right or *non*, if the child is wrong.

12. Use slide 20 of the PPT or use the flashcards with pictures only. Call out the names of the parts of the body again, pointing to that part as you go. Ask the children to work with a partner. One child calls out a part of the body, his/her partner points at it then they swap around. Give this activity a good five minutes, as it is a great opportunity for you to walk around and model pronunciation and support less confident pupils or just 'take the pulse' of the lesson.

Extension A

To finish the lesson on an energetic note, play and sing along to the song again "*Tête, épaules, genoux et pied*".

Click on the link in the PPT (slide 21):
https://www.youtube.com/watch?v=pgXXTWKjk-Q

Extension B

"*Alouette, gentille alouette*".
This is a song the pupils will absolutely love!
Explain that "*alouette*" is a bird, so it is not going to have "*une bouche*", but "*un bec*" (a beak).
After watching the video and listening to the song, play it one more time. The children can join in singing and pointing at different body parts. It's great fun!

Click on the link in the PPT (slide 22):
https://www.youtube.com/watch?v=L_hFw_cWg9U

French is Fun at Key Stage 1 © Brilliant Publications Limited

12. Family members

Introduction

Share the learning intention with the class and tell them that today you have some new little friends who have come to visit: a finger family. Show each finger puppet and ask the pupils to say which family member this could be.

Learning objectives

To learn the names for family members in French.

Vocabulary

ma famille	my family
mon papa	my dad
ma maman	my mum
ma sœur/ mes sœurs	my sister(s)
mon frère/ mes frères	my brother(s)
mon grand-père	my grandad
ma grand-mère	my grandma
C'est qui ?	Who is this?
Montrez-moi …	Show me …
J'ai … sœur(s)	I have … sister(s)
Je n'ai pas de sœurs	I don't have any sisters
J'ai … frère(s)	I have … brother(s)
Je n'ai pas de frères	I don't have any brothers

On the USB Drive

PPT presentation includes:
- family members with pictures only (slides 3–9)
- family members with words and pictures (slides 10–16)
- question and answers (slides 17–22)

Additional resources needed

Flashcards from the PPT (slides 3–16)
Small flashcards of family members (pages 101–103)
Finger puppets
Soft ball
Puppets
Small bag/ box

Activities

1. Using the PPT (slides 3–9) or flashcards with pictures only, introduce the new vocabulary through the *écoutez et répétez* activity. Repeat the activity, using words and pictures this time (slides 10–16). Note: *mon papa* and *ma maman* are used (as opposed to *mon père* and *ma mère*) because these are much apprpriate for children of this age and these words are used in the song.

ma famille

© Brilliant Publications Limited

French is Fun at Key Stage 1

2. Depending on the age and abilities of your pupils, you might like to explain that *mon, ma* and *mes* mean 'my' in French. Repeat the vocabulary again with the help of the little puppets. It is easier if you keep the males on one hand and the females on the other. Give names to each family member. Greet them with different greetings.

Start by asking:

Comment t'appelles-tu ? or
Comment ça va ?

eg. *ma maman –*   *Comment t'appelles-tu ?*

                              Je m'appelle Marie.

    mon papa –   *Comment t'appelles-tu ?*

                              Je m'appelle Pierre.

    ma sœur –   *Comment ça va ?*

                              Ca va très bien, merci.

3. Using the PPT, ask the class to only listen this time and try to remember as many family members as possible. After calling out the vocabulary a few times (use different voices and tones, clapping hands, etc.) show one little puppet and ask *C'est qui ?* (Who is this?) The pupils answer raising their hands.

4. Counting down from 5 to 0, ask the pupils to sit in a circle on the carpet. As we move a lot in our lesson, I usually offer little rewards (stickers, house point etc) if the pupils can follow the instructions quickly and quietly. Always stay in the middle of the circle and start by calling out the target vocabulary, asking the class to repeat. Give them a soft ball. The pupils can pass the ball from one to another, calling out different family members.

5. Divide the class in small groups (4–5 children) and give them a set of small flashcards, either with words or without (pages 101–103). Ask each group to put the cards on the floor, picture-side face up. Give them a few minutes to work in their teams, trying to remember the name of each family member – walk around, ready to help and offer your support if needed. The teacher now calls out *Montrez moi … ma maman/mon papa/ mon grand-père / ma grand-mère/ ma sœur/ mon frère* and each team must hold up the correct card. Remind the pupils that they are working as a team, so it doesn't matter which member of the team holds up the card, as long as it is the correct one.

6. Hide some cards around the room. Ask the class to remain in teams and tell the pupils that you have hidden around the class the same cards they have just used in the previous activity. Send one team at a time to search for some cards and give them 15–20 seconds. Count down in French, holding your hands up in the air so the children can

mon père

ma mère

ma sœur

mon frère

mon grand-père

ma grand-mère

French is Fun at Key Stage 1   © Brilliant Publications Limited

see as well as hear how many seconds remain. If they find a card or more, they must call out the name(s) of the family member(s) in the pictures then return to the carpet. Another team is nominated now to search, until each team has had a go.

7. Introduce the question *Tu as des frères ou des sœurs ?* (PPT slides 17–22) (Do you have brothers or sisters?) Explain that *j'ai* means 'I have' and *je n'ai pas* means 'I don't have'. Using your talking puppets, practise a short conversation. Afterwards ask the class how many brothers and sisters each puppet has.

8. Now ask the pupils the same question: *Tu as des frères ou des sœurs ?* (Do you have brothers or sisters?) As this is a difficult question to answer because the children need to remember how to use sentences with 'I have/ I don't have', make sure you use visual support on the IWB and that you practised *J'ai/ Je n'ai pas* beforehand with the class.

9. Make a circle on the carpet and give each child a small flashcard of a family member. Give the pupils 2–3 minutes to talk to their partner, trying to remember the names of the family member they have in their hands. Clap hands when you want them to stop. Walk around with a small bag/box and collect the cards. Each child must say which family member is in the picture he/she holds before putting it in your bag.

10. Return to the carpet spaces. Hold up a big flashcard and ask the class *C'est qui ?* (Who is this?) When you finish, ask the pupils to close their eyes for one minute and think about what they have learnt today.

Can they recall two family members/ three family members, etc?

Extension

'*Papa petit doigt*' song.

Click on the link in the PPT (slide 23):

https://www.youtube.com/watch?v=qjWMR76owOk

Watch and listen to the song first. Ask the children if they know which song this is in English. Most of them will recognise immediately the 'Daddy finger' song:

Daddy finger, daddy finger

Where are you?

Here I am, here I am,

How do you do?

Explain that the song is exactly the same in French. Practise each line with the class, asking them to stand up. Use actions and mimes for each line and make sure you ask the children to use only their right and left index finger for each family member. Always model the actions for the songs and do not be afraid to join in. The children will have great fun with this song and we often perform this in school assemblies, in front of their older peers.

© Brilliant Publications Limited

French is Fun at Key Stage 1

— Bonjour, Pointé !
— Comment ça va ?
— Comme ci, comme ça.
— Pointé, as-tu des frères ou des sœurs ?
— Je n'ai pas de frères et sœurs.
— Au revoir !

— Salut, Rose !
— Ça va bien, merci ! Et toi ?
— J'ai une sœur et deux frères. Et toi ?
— Au revoir !

13. Vegetables

Introduction

Greet the class and introduce the new lesson. Ask the pupils if they can remember the names of any fruit they learnt from before. After revising the names of the different fruit, give the children a chance to discuss with their partners which vegetables they might learn the names of today. Show them the big flashcards with pictures only and ask the pupils to name each vegetable in English.

Learning objectives

To learn the names of different types of vegetables in French.

Vocabulary

la carotte	the carrot
le concombre	the cucumber
la tomate	the tomato
le brocoli	the broccoli
le poivron	the pepper
le chou	the cabbage
le chou-fleur	the cauliflower
les petits pois	the peas
la pomme de terre	the potato
l'oignon	the onion
C'est quel légume ?	What vegetable is this?
Où est le/la/l' … ?	Where is the …?
Où sont les … ?	Where are the …?
Aimes-tu le/la/l'/les … ?	Do you like …?
J'aime le/la/l'/les …	I like …
Je n'aime pas le/la/l'/les …	I don't like …
J'adore le/la/l'/les …	I love …
Je déteste …	I don't like at all …

On the USB Drive

PPT presentation
- vegetables with pictures only (slides 3–12)
- vegetables with words and pictures (slides 13–22)

Additional resources needed

Flashcards from the PPT (slides 3–22)
Small flashcards of vegetables (one for each child) (pages 104–105)
Bag with plastic/fabric vegetables
Puppets
Soft ball

Activities

1. Start by introducing the French names through an *Écoutez et répétez* activity. First use the PPT (slides 3–12) flashcards with pictures only. Before introducing the spelling, remind the children that they need to listen carefully first, then they need to repeat exactly what they hear.

la carotte

© Brilliant Publications Limited   French is Fun at Key Stage 1

Use a variety of voices, tones, clapping hands, practising the target vocabulary as many times as possible.

2. Using the PPT presentation for visual support, repeat the new vocabulary asking the pupils to only listen this time. Show them the bag and take out one vegetable at a time. The teacher calls out the name of that vegetable and the pupils repeat it. Put everything back in the bag. Take each vegetable out again asking the class *C'est quel légume ?*

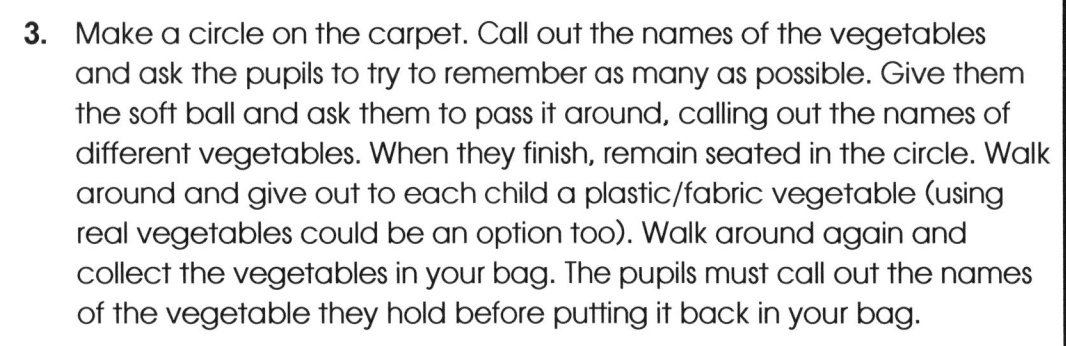

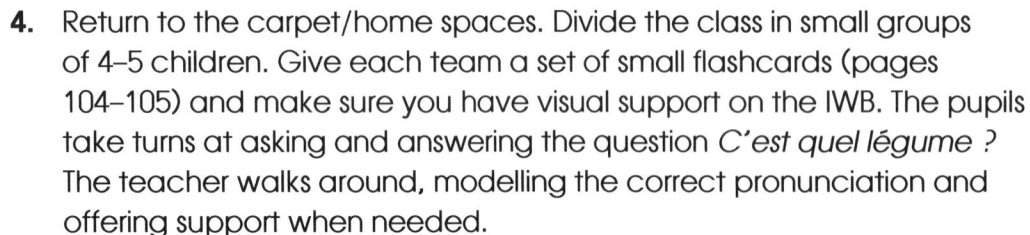

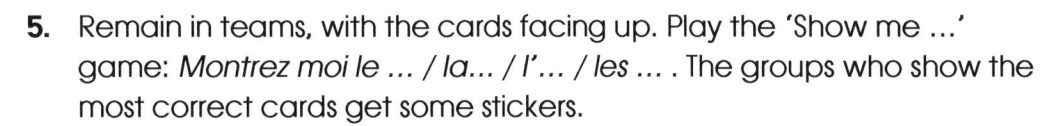

3. Make a circle on the carpet. Call out the names of the vegetables and ask the pupils to try to remember as many as possible. Give them the soft ball and ask them to pass it around, calling out the names of different vegetables. When they finish, remain seated in the circle. Walk around and give out to each child a plastic/fabric vegetable (using real vegetables could be an option too). Walk around again and collect the vegetables in your bag. The pupils must call out the names of the vegetable they hold before putting it back in your bag.

4. Return to the carpet/home spaces. Divide the class in small groups of 4–5 children. Give each team a set of small flashcards (pages 104–105) and make sure you have visual support on the IWB. The pupils take turns at asking and answering the question *C'est quel légume ?* The teacher walks around, modelling the correct pronunciation and offering support when needed.

5. Remain in teams, with the cards facing up. Play the 'Show me ...' game: *Montrez moi le ... / la... / l'... / les ...* . The groups who show the most correct cards get some stickers.

6. Freeze the PPT on slide 24 with all the vegetables. Play the 'Class versus teacher' game (see page 13). After playing the game 2–3 times, invite the children to raise their hands if they would like to come to the front and touch the correct picture when the teacher says *Où est le/la/l'...* + vegetable? (Where is the ... ?).

7. Keep the PPT frozen on slide 24. Invite two children to the front, facing the board. When you say *Touchez le/la/l'/les ...* (Touch the ...), the first pupil to touch the correct picture wins to play against another child. Try to permit each child to have a turn.

8. Play 'Guess the vegetable!' The children sit in a circle. The teacher walks around, outside the circle, and puts a plastic/fabric vegetable behind each pupil. The pupils can feel the vegetable, but they are not allowed to look. When the teacher comes around with the bag, the pupils try to guess which vegetable they are holding before putting it back in the bag.

9. Back to the carpet/home spaces. Recall the target vocabulary using visual support (PPT presentation or flashcards). Check with the class if they remember how to express likes or dislikes in French.

le concombre

la tomate

le poivron

le chou

le chou-fleur

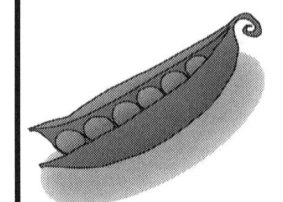

les petits pois

French is Fun at Key Stage 1

© Brilliant Publications Limited

The talking puppets will now chat about the vegetables they like or they don't like and the children must listen carefully. When the conversation finishes, ask the pupils which vegetables the puppets like or dislike.

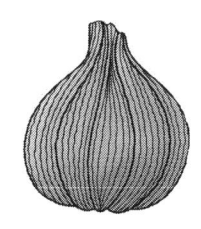

l'oignon

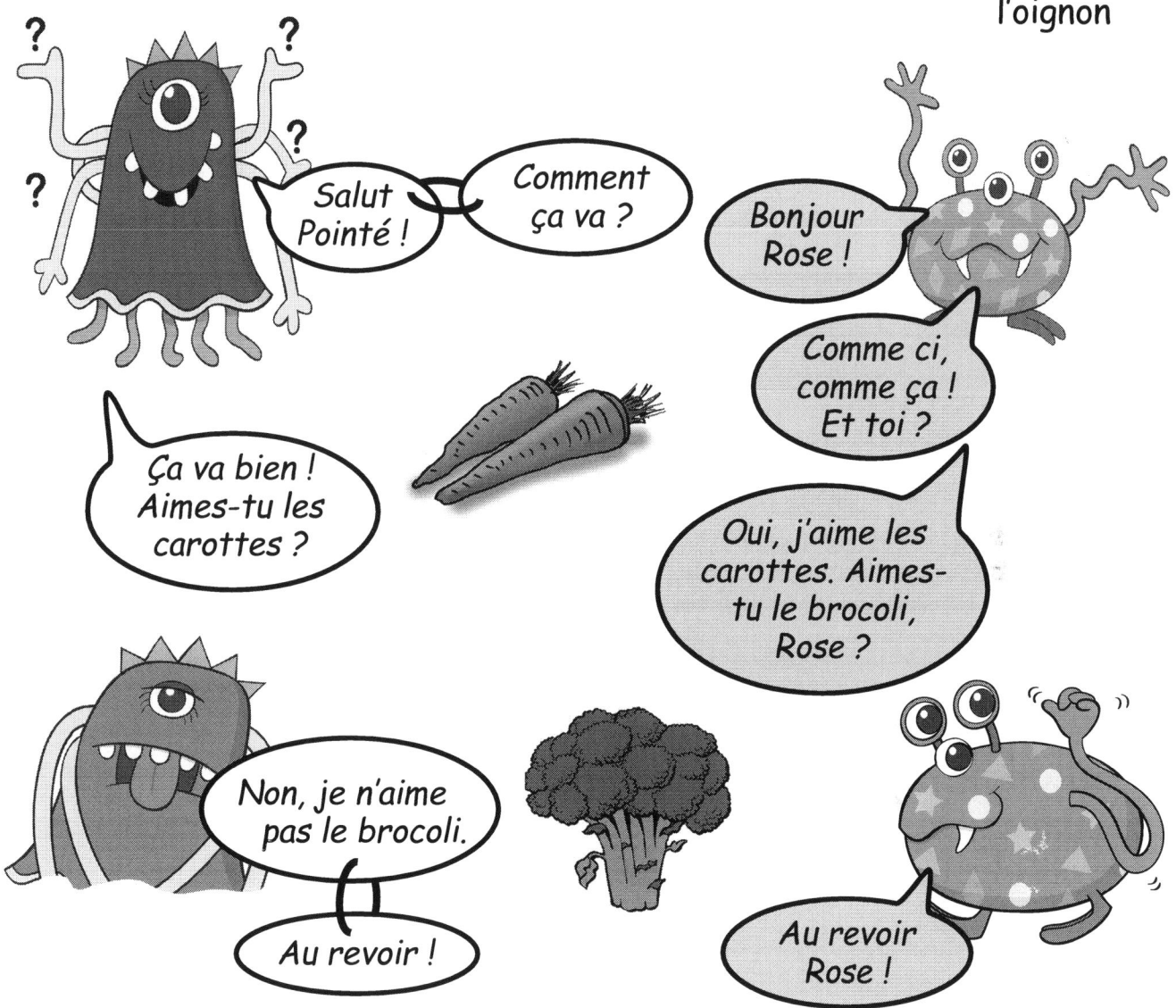

Salut Pointé !

Comment ça va ?

Bonjour Rose !

Comme ci, comme ça ! Et toi ?

Ça va bien ! Aimes-tu les carottes ?

Oui, j'aime les carottes. Aimes-tu le brocoli, Rose ?

Non, je n'aime pas le brocoli.

Au revoir !

Au revoir Rose !

10. Practise with the class different likes and dislikes. Get one of the talking puppets to 'walk' around and ask the pupils *Aimes-tu … + vegetable?* Encourage the pupils to respond and also ask back *Et toi ?*

11. Divide the class in small groups and give each child a small flashcard. Each child should look at their card, but not show the picture to the rest of the group. In teams, the pupils will try to guess what vegetable is on the other team members' cards. When they finish ask them to swap their cards with another group.

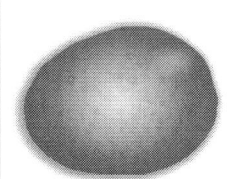

la pomme de terre

12. Return to the carpet/home spaces. Get the bag with vegetables and invite a more confident child to come to the front and put his/her hand in the bag, trying to feel and guess which vegetable they are holding. Ask *C'est quel légume ?* After the pupil answers, check if they are holding the correct vegetable and ask further questions: *Aimes-tu ... +* vegetable?

14. At the end of the lesson, ask the pupils to pair up with a partner. Each child will ask their partner how many vegetables they know in French. Encourage them to count in French. Give them one minute, then stop. The pupils who did the counting must show on their fingers how many vegetables their partner knows. Swap around and give them another minute for the same activity. The rest of the pupils can now show you how many vegetables their partner knows.

le brocoli

14. Classroom instructions

Introduction

The reason for leaving this topic last is a very simple one: you might choose not to teach this as a whole lesson, but just to introduce different instructions in every other lesson. For example, I teach *'écoutez et répétez'* and *'silence, s'il vous plaît'* in my very first lesson.

I have created a rhyme that I often use when I want the class to get ready for a new lesson or when I stop an activity, for transition between activities or when I need to get the pupils' full attention.

If you choose to teach the instructions as a lesson, here are some ideas of how you could do this.

Learning objectives
To learn simple classroom instructions in French.

Vocabulary

écoutez	listen
regardez	look
répétez	repeat
levez-vous	get up
asseyez-vous	sit down
mettez-vous en rang	line up
arrêtez	stop
mettez-vous en cercle	get in a circle
silence	be quiet
s'il vous plaît	please (plural)

On the USB Drive

PPT presentation includes:
- instructions with pictures only (slides 3–12)
- instructions with words and pictures (slides 13–22)

Additional resources needed

Flashcards from the PPT (slides 3–22)
Small flashcards with words only (pages 106–107)
Small bag

Activities

1. After introducing the new lesson, ask the children what a classroom instruction is and ask them to give you some examples. Get ready with mimes/actions for each instruction, but also with flashcards and pictures. The pupils might remember some instructions you have previously used in the lessons so you could ask them if they can give examples of instructions they know already in French.

2. Show the flashcards made from the PPT (slides 3–12), discuss with the class which instruction each picture might represent. Start practising the target vocabulary in French with short instructions such as *écoutez et répétez*! I introduce the instruction as a whole phrase. However, with longer instructions as *mettez-vous en cercle* or *mettez-vous en rang*, it helps to break them in short sequences when practising:

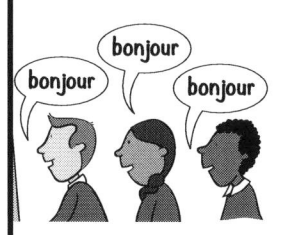

écoutez

répétez

© Brilliant Publications Limited

French is Fun at Key Stage 1

Me-ttez (clap-clap)
mettez (clap-clap)
vous (clap)
Me-ttez-vous (clap-clap-clap)
en (clap)
cer-cle (clap clap)
Me-ttez-vous (clap-clap-clap)
en cer-cle (clap-clap-clap)

3. As some instructions are quite difficult, the aim of the lesson is to make the class able to recognize and follow them, rather than learn them by heart. Go through the vocabulary again, using different voices and tones, clapping hands, actions and mimes. Play with *levez-vous/ asseyez-vous* – doing the actions. This will bring lots of laughter, especially if you repeat the same instruction twice in a row: *Levez-vous, asseyez-vous. Levez-vous, asseyez-vous. Levez-vous, asseyez-vous. Levez-vous, levez-vous.* At this point, a lot of children will sit down, because they expected the instruction to be *asseyez-vous*. Repeat the activity, asking the pupils to listen carefully and follow your instructions exactly: *Levez-vous, asseyez-vous. Levez-vous, asseyez-vous. Levez-vous, asseyez-vous. Asseyez-vous.*

4. Asking the class just to listen for now, use the PPT and go through the vocabulary (slides 13–22). The pupils must now follow your instructions, so listen carefully! Give them different instructions, for example '*Mettez-vous en cercle*', they have to sit in a circle, if the instruction is: '*levez-vous*', they should stand up, for '*silence*' they should stop any chatter and be silent, etc.

5. Ask the class to stand up, copy your actions and repeat the instructions after you. Model the action and the pronunciation of the instruction several times, then invite a more confident child to come to the front to mime an action. The rest of the class must say which instruction this is.

6. Sit the pupils in small groups of 3–4 and give them a small bag (or a plastic cup) with small laminated instruction cards. Call out an instruction. The group should hold up the card to match with your instruction.

7. Using the PPT presentation, go through each slide and practise one more time, with actions, mimes and the new vocabulary. Let the pupils know that today they will learn a rhyme which you are going to use in future lessons. Read the rhyme on slide 23 out loud and explain that you will always say the black lines and the class, the red lines.

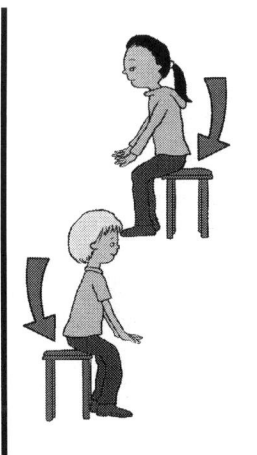

asseyez-vous

levez-vous

mettez-vous en rang

arrêtez

French is Fun at Key Stage 1

© Brilliant Publications Limited

Teacher: Un, deux, trois	Class: Comment ça va ?
Teacher: Un, deux, trois	Class: Comme ci, comme ça !
Teacher: Un, deux, trois	Class: Régardez !
Teacher: Un, deux, trois	Class: Écoutez !
Teacher: Un, deux, trois	Class: Répétez !
Teacher: Un, deux, trois	

All: <u>Arrêtez !</u>

For the first couple of times when you use the rhyme in class, join in with the class lines as well, to help children remember the order. It is easier to remember if they use actions. After a few practises you can just say the numbers and show the class the actions for the instruction they have to say.

silence

Au revoir

Why do we teach a modern foreign language in primary schools? I will try to create a picture of why and, most importantly, how we teach a foreign language in EYFS and KS1 and what the consequences are.

When I finished my studies at university, I went straight into teaching. I come from a family where this job is quite familiar; my older sister is a teacher, my aunty and my mother-in-law are teachers too. However, teaching was a challenge at that time especially being very young. I decided to teach MFL at a college; the age group I taught was 14 to 18-year-olds. Being just a couple of years older than my students, teaching French to adolescents seemed a great thing to do as I could easily relate my subject with their interests and mine too – music, sport, social media. (I was lucky enough to experience this when social media was still quite limited and it seemed to be a positive thing, rather than a seemingly negative one as nowadays.) But there came a moment in my life when I realised that I had to try all aspects of teaching, so I decided to teach primary children. I am not going to say that primary is better than secondary or college; each age group comes with its challenges, peculiarities and beauty. In one word, I would name this as 'flavour'. Yes, each age has its flavour that you can experiment with on both sides, as a student and as a teacher.

With primary pupils – starting with reception – my journey had totally new dimensions. I have been teaching in primary schools since 2006 and I still enjoy doing it. But the aim of this chapter is to look at some questions. The first one is why should a child learn a modern language at such a young age? When I am asked this question by an adult, I smile and just say "because we CAN". The brain is a muscle, it should be trained in many ways, with every opportunity we get. When learning a language, it is not only about learning new words or phrases but also about discovering the world around us. Geography, history, maths, science, music, English – these and many more are included in just three letters: MFL. The younger the learners are, the better they will receive and remember new things.

But how do we teach a modern foreign language effectively in EYFS and KS1? I have learnt from experience a few things that I am going to share with you here:

1. Probably the most important fact to remember is that your little pupils are beginners in everything, including English. The good part is that they won't be afraid to accept easily any new language (at an early age, pupils are able to reproduce the sounds with nearly or even similar accent as a native person would do). The tricky part is that you must carefully plan your lessons, with plenty of games, activities and repetition. As long as you can think from a perspective of a 5-year-old, you are safe. Don't be afraid to let the child inside you be playful.

2. With every new lesson, take your pupils on a journey: "Are you ready for a new trip? There is a new adventure waiting for us today – do you like adventures? OK, let's put on our imaginary hat/glasses. *Trois, deux, un ...* . Today we will visit planet numbers/ planet days/ planet colours," etc. There is nothing more powerful in a class than exciting the curiosity of your learners.

3. Start the lesson with something they love. I have some songs that I have taught with great success among my little ones; we choose one song and the pupils are free to dance and laugh. It is a nice warm up for the lesson; it's also a funny and engaging way to revise old vocabulary without actually letting the children know they are doing this.

4. Don't keep the pupils on the same activity/in the same place for more than 10 minutes! Use your classroom: charts, carpet, tables, chairs, coloured pencils, pictures, doors, windows, magnetic numbers, etc. Everything is useful when teaching a certain topic: numbers, colours, classroom instructions, days, months. Play with all of them: *Montrez-moi ...* (show me), *Touchez ...* (touch …). It is a good way to make them move around the classroom and keep their attention awake.

5. If your lesson implies an extra activity, do it in the target language. For example, I sit with my Year 1 class during their snack. So, we name the fruits in French; of course, I always remind them to *Lavez les mains* (Wash your hands) – it is part of the job. I go around and ask politely: *Une pomme ou une banane, mademoiselle/monsieur?/ Une poire ou une carotte, mademoiselle/monsieur?* and my pupils answer with their very best pronunciation: *Une pomme/banane/carotte, s'il vous plait* or with *Non, merci, madame.*

6. Once you have taught the greetings, use your language in any context that allows you to. We greet each other in French in the playground or in the corridors. Sometimes I stop for a little conversation, asking them different things about the topics we've learnt. Just a simple *Bonjour, William. Comment ca va ?* is a boost of confidence for your pupils. Just by being able to understand and answer your question(s), the children feel so appreciated for their effort.

7. This might not be your go to teaching tool but, believe me, talking puppets are one of my best methods to use in KS1. I have three of them: a cat, a dog and a frog. They are French (of course!) and my pupils are always keen to have a chat with them, no matter what topic we are learning. I cannot count in numbers how many hugs or kisses they have received from tiny people able to love a puppet in a way an adult wouldn't ever understand.

I am sure there are many other methods to teach a modern language during the early years and KS1, but whatever you use, don't forget that, beyond everything else, you should be ready every day to: tie up some shoe laces, wipe some tears and some little noses, smile a lot and, most of all, show love and kindness. The children grow up looking at their teachers and the adults in their life. It is our responsibility, no matter what subject we teach, to help them grow beautifully.

Greetings

French is Fun at Key Stage 1

© Brilliant Publications Limited

54

Greetings

© Brilliant Publications Limited

French is Fun at Key Stage 1

55

Greetings

French is Fun at Key Stage 1

© Brilliant Publications Limited

Greetings

French is Fun at Key Stage 1

Greetings

Greetings

Bonjour ! / Salut !	Bonjour ! / Salut !
Comment ça va ?	Comment ça va ?

Greetings

Ça va bien !	Ça va bien !
Ça va très bien !	Ça va très bien !

French is Fun at Key Stage 1

Greetings

Comme ci, comme ça	Comme ci, comme ça
Ça va mal !	Ça va mal !

Greetings

Ça va très mal !

Ça va très mal !

Désolée

Désolé

Greetings

| Au revoir ! | Au revoir ! |

Introducing yourself

Comment t'appelles-tu ?

Comment t'appelles-tu ?

Je m'appelle Rose.

Je m'appelle Pointé.

Numbers 0 to 10

Numbers 0 to 10

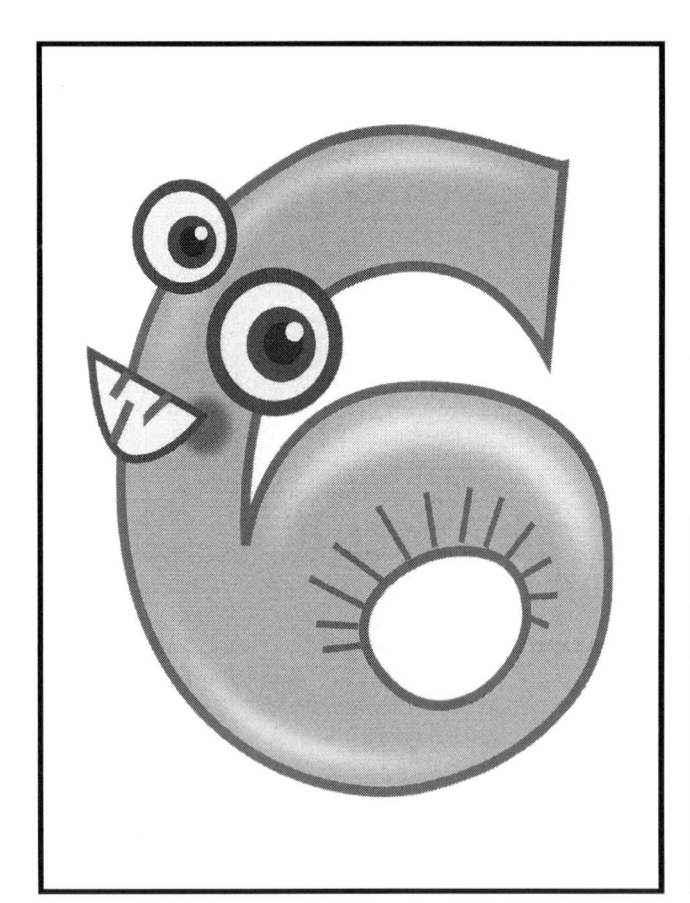

French is Fun at Key Stage 1

Numbers 0 to 10

French is Fun at Key Stage 1

Numbers 0 to 10

zéro	un
deux	trois

Numbers 0 to 10

| quatre | cinq |
| six | sept |

Numbers 0 to 10

huit	neuf
dix	

How old are you?

1	2
3	4
5	6

How old are you?

7	8
9	10

How old are you?

1 J'ai <u>un</u> an.

2 J'ai <u>deux</u> ans.

3 J'ai <u>trois</u> ans.

4 J'ai <u>quatre</u> ans.

5 J'ai <u>cinq</u> ans.

6 J'ai <u>six</u> ans.

© Brilliant Publications Limited

French is Fun at Key Stage 1

How old are you?

7 J'ai <u>sept</u> ans.	**8** J'ai <u>huit</u> ans.
9 J'ai <u>neuf</u> ans.	**10** J'ai <u>dix</u> ans.

Numbers 11 to 20

Numbers 11 to 20

Numbers 11 to 20

onze	douze
treize	quatorze
quinze	seize

Numbers 11 to 20

dix-sept	dix-huit
dix-neuf	vingt

Colours

French is Fun at Key Stage 1

79

Colours

Colours

rouge	bleu
orange	jaune
violet	rose

Colours

marron	vert
noir	blanc
gris	

French is Fun at Key Stage 1 © Brilliant Publications Limited

Colours

rouge

bleu

orange

jaune

Colours

violet

rose

marron

vert

Colours

noir

blanc

gris

The Days of the Week

lundi	vendredi
mardi	samedi
mercredi	dimanche
jeudi	

The Days of the Week

lun	di	vendre	di
mar	di	same	di
mercre	di	di	manche
jeu	di		

Florentina Popescu

French is Fun at Key Stage 1

Animals and pets

French is Fun at Key Stage 1

Animals and pets

Animals and pets

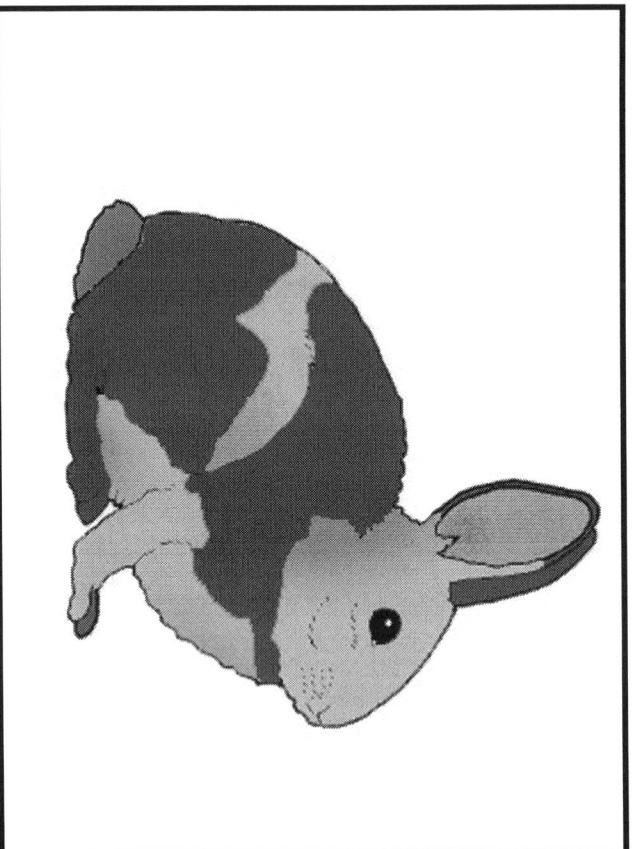

French is Fun at Key Stage 1

© Brilliant Publications Limited

Animals and pets

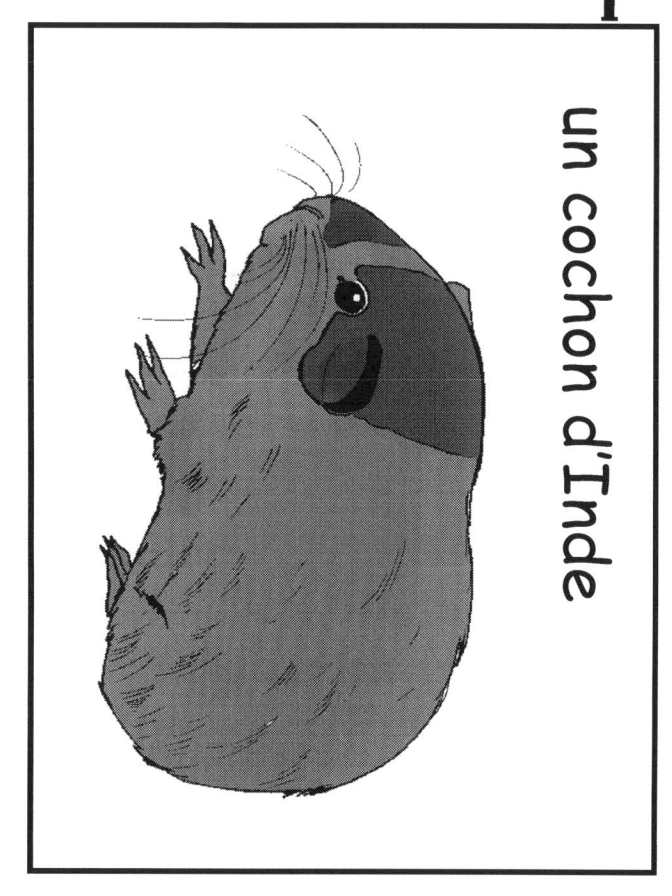

un cochon d'Inde

une tortue

un poisson

un chien

Animals and pets

un chat

un oiseau

une araignée

une souris

Animals and pets

un serpent

un lapin

Fruits

French is Fun at Key Stage 1

94

© Brilliant Publications Limited

Fruits

Fruits

la fraise

la pomme

la banane

l'orange

Fruits

l'ananas

la pêche

la cerise

la poire

Months of the year

janvier	juillet
février	août
mars	septembre
avril	octobre
mai	novembre
juin	décembre

janvier	juillet
février	août
mars	septembre
avril	octobre
mai	novembre
juin	décembre

janvier	juillet
février	août
mars	septembre
avril	octobre
mai	novembre
juin	décembre

janvier	juillet
février	août
mars	septembre
avril	octobre
mai	novembre
juin	décembre

French is Fun at Key Stage 1 — Florentina Popescu

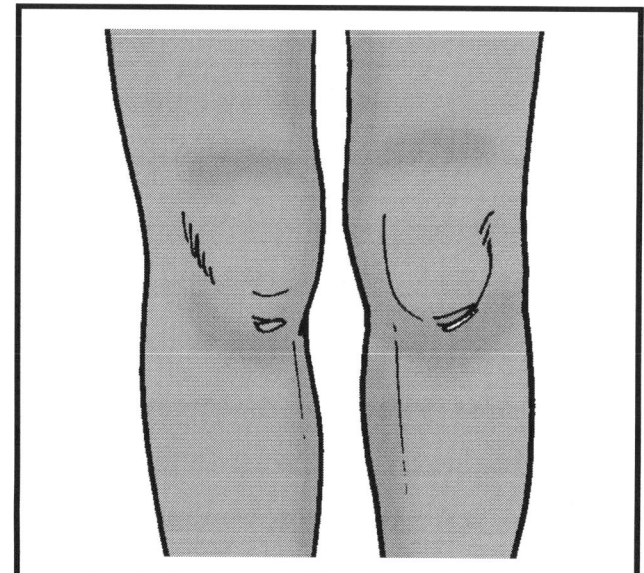

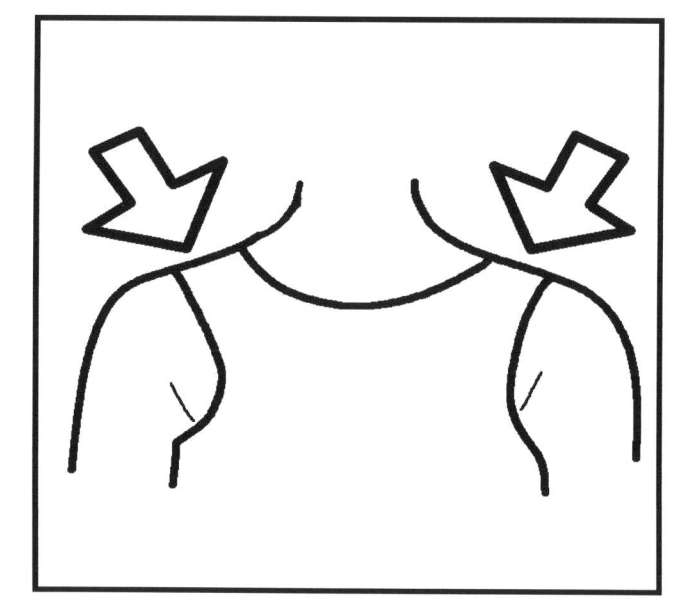

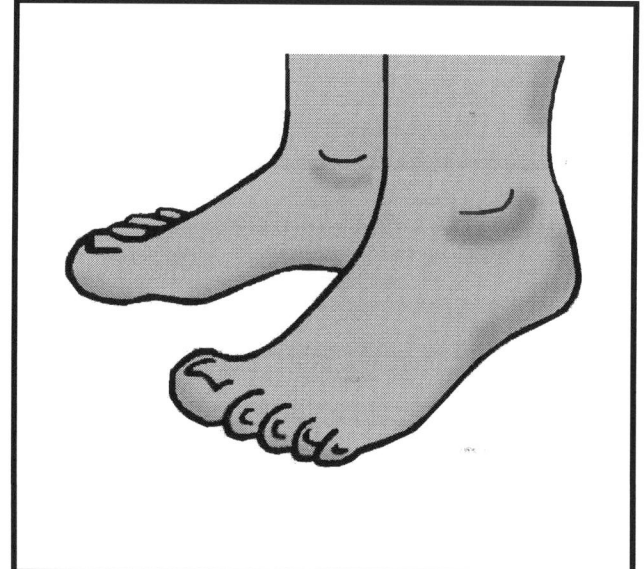

Body parts

Body parts

Family members

mon père

ma mère

ma sœur

mon frère

French is Fun at Key Stage 1

Family members

mon grand-père

ma grand-mère

Family members

Vegetables

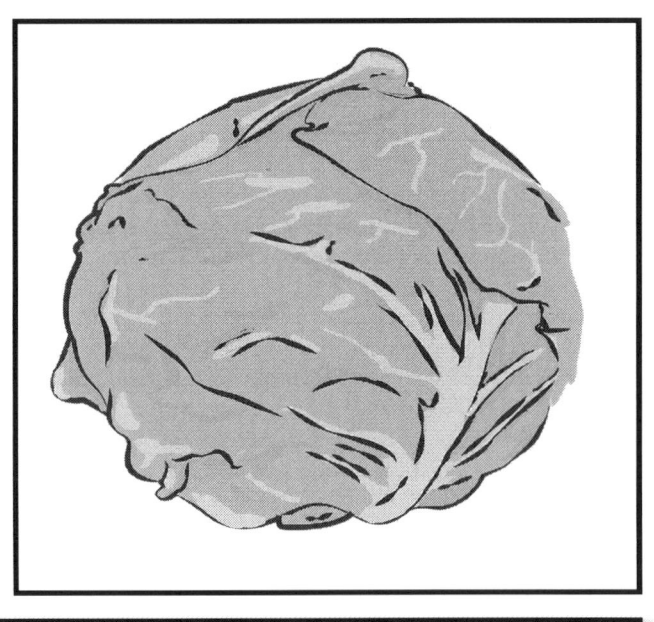

French is Fun at Key Stage 1

© Brilliant Publications Limited

104

Vegetables

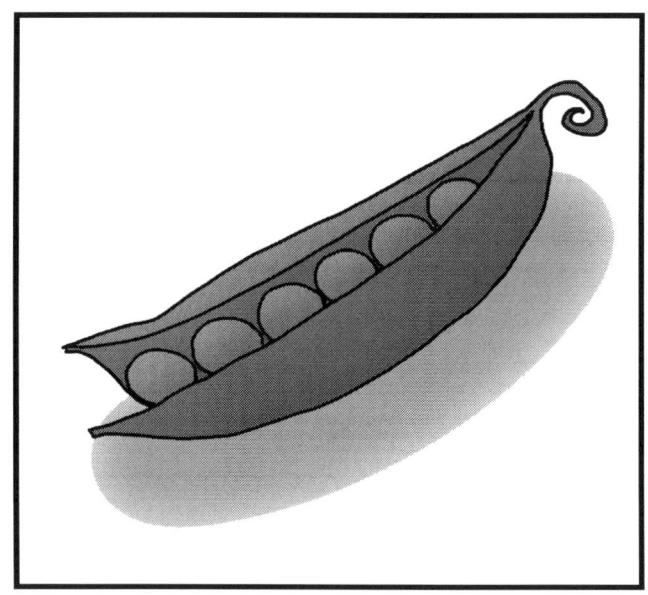

Classroom Instructions

Écoutez !	Levez-vous !
Répétez !	Silence !
Asseyez-vous !	Regardez !

French is Fun at Key Stage 1

© Brilliant Publications Limited

| Mettez-vous en cercle ! | Mettez-vous en rang ! |

Arrêtez